Reclaiming
Your Inner
Child

OTHER BOOKS IN THE MINIRTH-MEIER SERIES

The Anger Workbook
Dr. Les Carter, Dr. Frank Minirth

A Circle of Love
Guy Chandler, Laura A. Brown, Jane Swindell

Don't Let Jerks Get the Best of You
Dr. Paul Meier

The Father Book
Dr. Frank Minirth, Dr. Brian Newman, Dr. Paul
Warren

Imperative People
Dr. Les Carter

In Search of the Heart
Dr. David Allen

The Intimacy Factor
Dr. David Stoop, Jan Stoop

Intimate Moments
David & Teresa Ferguson, Chris & Holly Thurman

The Lies We Believe
Dr. Chris Thurman

Love Hunger: Recovery from Food Addiction
Dr. Frank Minirth, Dr. Paul Meier, Dr. Robert
Hemfelt, Dr. Sharon Sneed

Love Hunger Weight-Loss Workbook
Dr. Frank Minirth, Dr. Paul Meier, Dr. Robert
Hemfelt, Dr. Sharon Sneed

The Love Hunger Action Plan
Dr. Sharon Sneed

Love Is a Choice
Dr. Robert Hemfelt, Dr. Frank Minirth, Dr. Paul
Meier, Don Hawkins

Love Is a Choice Workbook
Dr. Robert Hemfelt, Dr. Frank Minirth, Dr. Paul
Meier, Dr. Brian Newman, Dr. Debbi Newman

Passages of Marriage
Dr. Frank Minirth, Mary Alice Minirth, Dr. Brian
Newman, Dr. Deborah Newman, Dr. Robert Hemfelt,
Susan Hemfelt

Passages of Marriage Series
New Love
New Love Study Guide
Realistic Love
Realistic Love Study Guide
Steadfast Love
Steadfast Love Study Guide
Renewing Love
Renewing Love Study Guide
Transcendent Love
Transcendent Love Study Guide
Dr. Frank & Mary Alice Minirth, Drs. Brian &
Deborah Newman, Dr. Robert & Susan Hemfelt

The Path to Serenity
Dr. Robert Hemfelt, Dr. Frank Minirth, Dr. Richard
Fowler, Dr. Paul Meier

Please Let Me Know You, God
Dr. Larry Stephens

The Quest
Kevin Brown, Ray Mitsch

Reclaiming Your Inner Child Workbook
Ken Parker

Steps to a New Beginning
Sam Shoemaker, Dr. Frank Minirth, Dr. Richard
Fowler, Dr. Brian Newman, Dave Carder

The Thin Disguise
Pam Vredevelt, Dr. Deborah Newman, Harry Beverly,
Dr. Frank Minirth

Things That Go Bump in the Night
Dr. Paul Warren, Dr. Frank Minirth

*The Twelve Best Kept Secrets for Living an Emotionally
Healthy Life*
Dr. Chris Thurman

What They Didn't Teach You in Seminary
Dr. Paul Meier, Dr. Frank Minirth, Dr. David Congo,
Dr. Brian Newman, Dr. Richard Meier, Dr. Allen
Doran

For general information about other Minirth-Meier Clinic branch offices, counseling services, educational resources and hospital programs, call toll-free 1-800-545-1819. National Headquarters: 214-669-1733 or 800-229-3000.

Reclaiming *Your Inner* Child

A
JANET
THOMA
BOOK

Thomas Nelson Publishers
Nashville

Published in Nashville, Tennessee, by Thomas Nelson, Inc., and distributed in Canada by Word
Communications, Ltd., Richmond, British Columbia, and in the United Kingdom by Word (UK),
Ltd., Milton Keynes, England.

Scripture quotations are from the NEW KING JAMES VERSION of the Bible. Copyright ©
1979, 1980, 1982, Thomas Nelson, Inc., Publishers.

The stories of the characters in this workbook are based on composites of numerous patients
seen by Kenneth Parker and his associates. The incidence of any names or events bearing
resemblance to those of actual people is coincidental.

ISBN: 0-8407-4332-7

Printed in the United States of America

1 2 3 4 5 6 — 98 97 96 95 94 93

Contents

Acknowledgments

To my wife, Mary Jo, and my children, Wayne Shoquist, Laurie McConnell, and Mandi Parker. Thank you for your inspiration as well as your patience.

Thank you, Catharine Walkinshaw, for putting words to the concepts and thoughts. Thank you, Janet Thoma, for having faith in me and putting up with my novice questions in the early days of this project. And thanks to the excellent editorial staff at Thomas Nelson Publishers.

Thank you, Lord, for giving me the gift that made this whole project possible.

And finally, thanks to you, my patients. I have learned so much from you through my years of practicing psychotherapy. You had the courage to make the journey to recovery. You had the courage to pick up the phone and ask someone for help. You have been my greatest teacher and I love you all.

LEARNING AND RECOVERING

Step One

Starting Out

Sally Dansen had everything any woman could want—a loving husband, two wonderful children, a beautiful home, friends—but Sally _didn't_ have everything she wanted. She wasn't happy, and she didn't know why.

Phil Sanderling had tried every treatment and therapy he'd heard about. His problem wasn't depression, he just couldn't make a commitment to a relationship. Every time he got close to a girl and she started talking marriage, he ran the other way. His latest girlfriend was really special to him. He didn't want to drive this one away, too, so he decided to talk to a counselor.

Going Deeper

When people come to me at the Minirth-Meier Tunnell and Wilson Clinic, it's usually because they sense something is wrong, something amiss that they can't finger. They've tried other conventional therapies and counseling, all with no lasting results.

I believe that inside each of us, whether we're eighteen or eighty-one, beats the heart of a tiny, special being—an inner child. This was the being who came into the world at our birth, and we've kept this inner child with us as we've matured.

Sometimes through childhood experiences, this inner child is injured. As we grow into adults, this injury starts to surface in ways that create problems for us.

"I don't know what else I can do," Dave Dansen, Sally's husband, told me. "I've given Sally every material possession she's wanted. She's been to counseling—her best friend has even tried to help. But Sally's still not happy. Now things have gotten out of hand. God knows I love her, but she's bringing me down too—and the kids. It's the kids I'm worried about the most. I heard your radio program the other day and decided to give you a call. We've tried just about everything else and nothing's worked."

"What sort of things worry you about Sally?" I asked Dave.

"She hardly ever leaves the house now. Sally's afraid to be in a crowd. She won't sleep at night unless we keep a light on. She's even afraid of thunderstorms. These phobias of hers have gotten out of hand."

The Juggling Act

We've all seen a street juggler at the fair. He throws one ball up, then another, then another, and then some more. The more skilled the juggler, the more balls in the air, and the higher the risk. The crowd appeal of his act increases with the number of balls soaring above him. But if one ball falls, the juggler's concentration is interrupted and he has a greater chance of losing more.

Many times life feels like a juggling act. We try to balance a demanding job, busy home life, kids, a wife or husband, ourselves, church, and all the other activities we get involved in. It feels like we're trying to keep all the balls in the air. Sometimes they stay there, sometimes they don't. And, like the juggler, the more balls that fall, the more likely the rest are to drop, a domino effect. In 90 percent of the cases I see, these surface problems are actually symptoms of a wounded inner child. Such was the case with Sally Dansen.

Symptoms of a Wounded Inner Child

Look over the following list and see if any of these symptoms sound familiar to you or someone you know.

1. ____ Depression

   Do you have periods of unhappiness that come and go without any logical reason? Are you unhappy more than you are happy? Recurring depression or a long history of depression is particularly significant.

2. ____ Moodiness

   Do you have frequent changes in moods? One minute you're very up, high on life; the next you're down in the dumps, on the bottom.

3. ____ Anxiety

   Do you suffer from nervous tension, sleeping difficulties, excessive worry, anxiety about job and family performance?

4. ____ Fears

   Are you afraid of things in everyday life (such as going outside the house, driving in traffic, being in a crowd, darkness, thunderstorms)? Do these fears lead to feelings of panic?

5. ____ Problems with Relationships

   Do you have trouble with your current relationship? Have you had frequent breakups?

6. ____ Perfectionism

   Are you unable to settle for a less-than-perfect standard in your various activities?

Frankly, I'd be surprised if you couldn't check at least one of these statements, for we've all experienced these symptoms at one time or another. People come to me for help when these symptoms have become so crippling they affect their everyday functioning.

"What seems to be the problem?" I asked Phil Sanderling at his first session.

Phil shifted in his chair. "Well, I seem to have this intense fear of commitment—commitment to a relationship. I'm thirty-five and would like to be married and have a family. But every time I meet the girl I think is right, I stop seeing her when we get serious. I'm here because I'm wondering now if it's my problem."

"Well, Phil, you've made an enormous first step. That is, looking to yourself and not to others for the problem. It's an excellent beginning. So this fear of a relationship is starting to affect your happiness? Is that right?" I asked.

"Exactly. I've met a new girl. Her name's Gina. We met at our church singles group. I really like her. She's different from anyone I've ever dated. And we share a lot with the Lord. I don't want to lose her, so I decided to see if you could help me."

As we will see, I used the Inner Child therapy to pursue and heal Phil's inner child, which had been injured during Phil's childhood and was now affecting his adult life. Yet, Phil never could come up with specific memories of childhood abuse or trauma. In fact he felt he had a happy and normal childhood. There wasn't anything he could recall that had injured his inner self.

I have found that many seemingly normal childhoods have actually caused subtle, but often detrimental, effects to the inner children of my clients. Some people do have normal childhoods and don't need counseling. Some childhoods, however, contain hidden negative messages which seem normal but can cause problems for adults.

Compulsive Behaviors

Inner child problems often show themselves as compulsive behaviors resulting from fear. Such was the case with Sally Dansen and Phil Sanderling.

A compulsive behavior is:

- repetitive—one you repeat over and over again;
- addictive—one you may swear off but will return to when under stress;
- self-destructive—although some compulsions may initially seem beneficial, in the long run, they actually harm you.

Phil feared intimacy. His flight from serious relationships had developed into a compulsion because he repeated this behavior with many women. He had come to the clinic for help when this behavior had started to become emotionally self-destructive.

Sally had several fears: crowds, darkness, thunderstorms. Her symptoms had developed into compulsions that were affecting her well-being, her marriage, and her family. During her sessions, she could check at least four of the following behaviors. How about you?

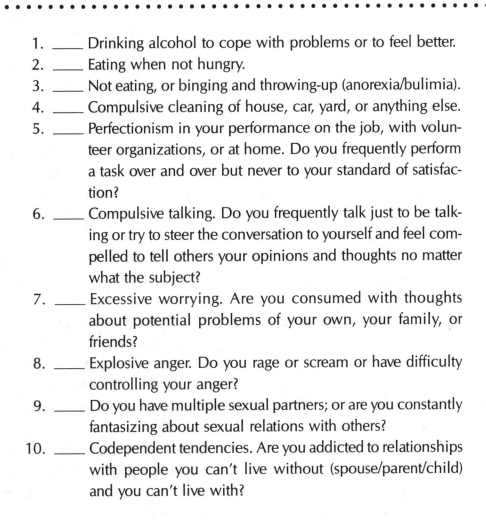

1. ____ Drinking alcohol to cope with problems or to feel better.
2. ____ Eating when not hungry.
3. ____ Not eating, or binging and throwing-up (anorexia/bulimia).
4. ____ Compulsive cleaning of house, car, yard, or anything else.
5. ____ Perfectionism in your performance on the job, with volunteer organizations, or at home. Do you frequently perform a task over and over but never to your standard of satisfaction?
6. ____ Compulsive talking. Do you frequently talk just to be talking or try to steer the conversation to yourself and feel compelled to tell others your opinions and thoughts no matter what the subject?
7. ____ Excessive worrying. Are you consumed with thoughts about potential problems of your own, your family, or friends?
8. ____ Explosive anger. Do you rage or scream or have difficulty controlling your anger?
9. ____ Do you have multiple sexual partners; or are you constantly fantasizing about sexual relations with others?
10. ____ Codependent tendencies. Are you addicted to relationships with people you can't live without (spouse/parent/child) and you can't live with?

11. ____ Drug abuse. This can also include prescription drugs. Do you have to use a prescription to sleep nearly every night?
12. ____ Panic Disorders. Are you afraid of being in crowds, in the dark, or of leaving the house? Has this fear kept you from doing some activities?
13. ____ Workaholism or drivenness. Do you spend long hours at your job or volunteer duties? Do you fill your day with appointments, meetings, work, and other activities leaving little or no leisure time?

• •

If you could check at least one of the above statements, you might be exhibiting some compulsions that are actually masking a deeper problem.

Or, you might be saying to yourself, *There's nothing wrong with me. I really don't have any of these symptoms or behaviors. Why do I need to discover my inner child? I don't really need this workbook.*

That might be the case, and if it is, I certainly applaud you. But this workbook is not just about problems. It's also about relationships. I will show you, through the Inner Child Model, how to improve relationships with yourself and those around you—your spouse, your children, your friends, whether those relationships are strained or not.

However, if you, like the majority of us, could check any of the above behaviors, I highly recommend you seek help for that compulsion, either through a support group, a professional counselor, or your pastor. Again, in 90 percent of these cases I see, these compulsions are not the problem. They are merely the ways the mind tries to cover up the problem. In fact, compulsions are the way we try to keep our inner selves hidden. And, they usually get much worse under stress as with Sally Dansen, who found her phobia of going out in a crowd was more pronounced when her schedule was particularly harried.

In this workbook I seek to go beneath the symptoms and compulsions to uncover the problem within and to resolve it. Just as a doctor will look at the symptoms of a patient and then order tests to find the cause of the symptoms, I also want to find the cause. Otherwise the inner problem will fester and rear its ugly head again, maybe in a whole new set of symptoms or problems.

This is why I usually receive clients who have found conventional therapy temporarily successful but then found themselves in need of help again. I will plumb the depths to discover the deeper problem.

But this takes time. To be lasting and complete, you will need to make a time commitment to this process. It can't be done in two or three days, over a weekend, or even in a week. That realization was especially hard for Phil Sanderling.

"You mean you can't give me some quick exercises to do, some fast techniques to solve my fears? I'm seeing Gina now and every day I'm afraid I'll blow it. I don't know if I can commit to do this."

That was something Phil had to decide for himself. Likewise you will have to make a commitment to yourself. Are you worth it?

I want you to think about this commitment to yourself before going further. See if you feel you are worth the time and effort it will take. Usually when I ask clients for a commitment, I have them put it in writing, in the form of a letter to themselves. Sally Dansen's letter read something like the following:

Dear Sally,

You don't know if Ken Parker has the answer or not, but you've reached the end of your rope. There's nowhere else to turn. Now, you might lose Dave and the kids. Is it worth that? No. God loves you and wants you happy. He works through many avenues to help you. Open up now and let Him work with you and make you better. You're worth it. Sign the following statement and plan to stick with it, through thick and thin, and trust in the Lord that it will work out for the best.

Sincerely,
Sally Dansen

I, Sally Dansen, promise to commit to work through this Inner Child process. I know it won't be easy. But I'm worth it and so is my family.

Sally Dansen   *Sept. 1, 1992*
_____   _____
Signature   Date

    Think now about your letter to yourself. What are the reasons you want to rediscover your inner child? What are the problems or anxieties you want resolved? What are the relationships you'd like to improve in your life today? Fill in the following blanks with your letter to yourself. This is the crucial first step toward acknowledging your inner child.

Dear _____,

_____

_____

_____

_____

_____

_____

_____

_____

_____

_____

                           Sincerely,

                           _____

Now that you've told yourself you're worth the attention, sign the following statement of commitment.

I, _____, promise to work through the Inner Child process. I know it won't be easy. But I'm worth it and so are my family and friends.

_____   _____
Signature   Date

Getting Started

This workbook is divided into two major parts. The first part explains the Inner Child Model and helps you meet and heal your inner child. The second part is a practical guide, with lots of information on how to use the Inner Child Model in your everyday life.

Each part is further divided into steps toward recovery and maintenance of your recovery. The steps are contained in chapters, filled with exercises. Each chapter builds on the next. For that reason, I recommend you go through the workbook, chapter by chapter, step by step.

I have been working in the psychotherapy field for over seventeen years. Along with the rest of the professional staff at the Minirth-Meier Tunnell and Wilson Clinic, I provide individual, family, and marital counseling. This Inner Child Model has evolved from my practice. With its application, I have had a very high success rate with my clients.

One of my most interesting cases is that of Ellen, a seventy-year-old woman, who came to me, desperately unhappy. As you will see in the following chapters, she rediscovered her inner child and was able to turn around her life for the better. It's never too late to find your child within.

As you go through this workbook, you may have questions about the exercises. Maybe you won't understand what I'm asking you to do. Perhaps you won't be able to come up with an answer. That's normal. Don't worry about unanswered questions. Upon completing the workbook you may have found your answers. We only have to worry when we stop asking the questions.

If your questions are overriding, ask someone for help. This workbook is not meant to take the place of a professional counselor or therapist. You may choose to use it in conjunction with a therapy group or counseling session. Whether you've chosen to use this book with such an arrangement or not, I highly recommend you set up a support network to help you through it—a trusted friend, your pastor, or a group.

Sally Dansen, fortunately, could rely on her husband, her best friend, her pastor, and me to help her. Think now of the people you can count on to support you as you go through the lessons in this workbook.

· ·

Friends/Family   Support Groups

_____   _____

_____   _____

_____   _____

_____   _____

_____   _____

_____   _____

_____   _____

_____   _____

· ·

Some of these exercises may bring up unpleasant thoughts and memories, or even pain. That's also normal. I feel I'm making headway when a patient experiences pain or anger. This means the layers are coming off around the inner child and progress is being made. Your support network will be necessary to get you through these rough times.

Throughout the exercises there will be lots of writing. Most therapists recognize the intrinsic value of writing for their patients since writing works as a catharsis. Somehow when you pull the thoughts and feelings out of your mind and put them down on paper, you feel better. They're no longer swirling around and muddling up your mind. Also, when these thoughts are down on paper, they surface to be resolved. In the mind, they are too diffuse to understand and deal with.

When writing for this book, don't bother with grammar, spelling, or punctuation. This isn't an English test. Just record the thoughts that first come to mind. And if some don't, use thought-provokers. What is it about my childhood I don't like? Why don't I want to think about it? Use these thoughts as triggers for your mind then write down whatever you think about next.

Because this will take concentration, commitment, and time, I recommend not trying to do more than one chapter a week. I also recommend setting aside a specific time and day each week to work with this book, preferably one when you won't be interrupted (like after the kids go to school or in the morning before anyone gets up).

When will you work on this workbook? Fill in the following blanks. Initially, Sally Dansen's time to use her workbook was Tuesdays from 9:00 A.M. to 11:00 A.M. How about yours?

_____   _____

    Day   Time

Be careful not to allow your work in this book to become another compulsion. Everyone knows that compulsive people can become compulsive with anything they get their hands on. (Have you ever noticed how vehement a former smoker is against smokers?) That's the addiction or compulsion working in the opposite direction. Of course, this is sometimes necessary to overcome a habit or problem. What I don't want, however, is for you to use this workbook as another thing to hold over yourself. Don't worry if you miss a week, or try to complete this workbook in one month. But keep in mind: I don't recommend that you put the workbook down for more than two weeks without progress.

Now make sure you put this book in a safe place, far away from the kids' crayons and others' curious eyes. It's yours and yours alone. Find someplace secret and special that only you know.

The First Step

You've already taken the first step by obtaining this book and working through the first chapter. That alone shows you care about yourself. The apostle Paul tells us that God cares about us also: "For I am persuaded that neither death nor life, nor angels nor principalities nor powers, nor things present nor things to come, nor height nor depth, nor any other created thing, shall be able to separate us from the love of God which is in Christ Jesus our Lord" (Rom. 8:38–39).

You can be secure that God will walk beside you in your journey, if you ask Him. You are safe in His love. You are a special person to Him. No matter what happens, He will be there for you.

Before beginning the next lesson, take a moment to think about how you feel so far. When Sally Dansen filled in this page, her thoughts looked something like the following:

"I feel scared and uneasy since I started this process, like something's deeply wrong and I'm afraid to find it. I don't know if I want to go on, but I'm committed to my family and to myself. The alternative is to continue with my unhappiness and I don't want that. So I guess I'm willing to take the risk and proceed."

How do you feel?

I feel _____ now that I've started this
workbook. Some other thoughts and feelings I'm having are: _____
_____
_____

The Inner Child Model

2

"What can you tell me about your childhood?" I asked Sally Dansen.

She sat across from me in my office. An attractive woman in her mid-thirties, she was slender, and had long, dark brown hair and expressive green eyes. Sally hugged herself and crossed her legs close to my couch.

"Well, it was pretty normal, I guess," she answered. "Mom stayed home with us kids. My dad traveled a lot. I had two brothers, a dog, and a cat. You know, normal stuff."

"Tell me about your dad," I said.

"To tell the truth, he wasn't around that much." She smiled. "He did send me flowers on my thirteenth birthday. I'll never forget it. They were pink roses. It was the first time I got flowers."

"How about your mother?"

"She was the typical mom, baked cookies for us, helped at the school. She was even my Brownie leader. She did all the cooking and cleaning. A very traditional mom."

"Did you feel loved by each of your parents?"

"Well, sure. I had all I needed—clothes, food. And they were interested in what I was doing. I guess I felt loved."

"How'd you feel about their relationship with each other?" I asked.

"They fought some, but they're still married. They never showed much affection to each other in front of us kids, but I'm sure they loved each other."

"And, was there anyone else who lived with you besides your mom, dad, and brothers?"

Sally shifted her position. "How come you're asking me all these questions about my past? It's the present that I'm having problems with, not my childhood."

"Sally, I hope to show you that what happens in our past, our childhood, has enormous impact on what happens today. So bear with me and try to answer these questions as best you can. I'm not out to find anything wrong with your childhood, I just need a little information so we can target your treatment. Sound okay?"

"I guess. Well, the only person that lived with us was my uncle. He moved in when I was in kindergarten."

"Can you tell me a little about him?"

"It was so long ago. I don't remember much about him. I still don't see what bearing this has on my current state of affairs. Don't you want to know about my husband and kids too?"

"Sure, tell me about them," I said.

Sally Dansen went on to tell me about her current family. She had two lovely children, eight-year-old Britney and ten-year-old Kevin. She talked on and on about their accomplishments. Dave, her husband, had a demanding job as a mid-level manager at a major insurance corporation. He spent extra hours at the office, something Sally disliked.

Every time I tried to steer the conversation back to Sally's childhood, she avoided the questions. As I confirmed later, this was a clue to something her mind was covering up. It alerted me that Sally might have an injured inner child.

What Is the Inner Child Model?

The Inner Child Model is a way of looking at your mind and its thoughts. I was not the first to develop this approach to psychotherapy. Nor will I be the last. Many well-respected psychologists use Inner Child therapy with extreme success today. However, I have added the dimension of the Christian perspective to this model. God makes an enormous investment in our inner child, as I will show you.

For now, though, let me explain what the Inner Child Model is. I don't have the room, nor do I want to expand this workbook into a primer for psychology, but I'll briefly define what the Inner Child Model is comprised of and what it means.

Developmental Theories

Developmental theories purport that a human being passes through various phases as he or she grows older: infancy, toddlerhood, young and late childhood, adolescence, young adulthood, middle age, and late life. In order to pass from one stage to the next, one has to master certain tasks or development standards. If done so successfully the door is closed on the former stage and opened to the next. If not, the last stage is returned to repeatedly until its tasks are mastered.

For instance, if individuation (the main task of adolescence) doesn't occur, the person will forever vacillate between dependence on others and rebellion against them.

The Inner Child Model

The Inner Child Model combines aspects of these development theories with analytical psychology. Tasks from each stage have to be mastered if a person is to develop into a healthy, functioning adult.

However, the Inner Child concept also operates on the premise that childhood experiences are carried over into adulthood. Thus, it differs from developmental theories because a door is never shut upon leaving a stage.

It also adds the aspects of psychoanalytical theories, which teach that there are two parts to the mind, the unconscious and the conscious, which are in constant conflict. The unconscious mind continually tries to bring its thoughts into the forefront of the conscious mind. And the conscious mind, with its defense mechanisms, tries to keep these thoughts (particularly if they are painful) suppressed. For the mind to allow such painful, unconscious thoughts to become conscious (in the active memory) would be to experience this pain all over again. The conscious mind does whatever it can to avoid pain.

In simpler terms, then, the Inner Child Model uses both developmental and psychoanalytical theories in a practical sense. Briefly, there are two basic parts to everyone's psyche: an inner child (or unconscious mind) and an outer self (conscious mind). It looks something like the following diagram.

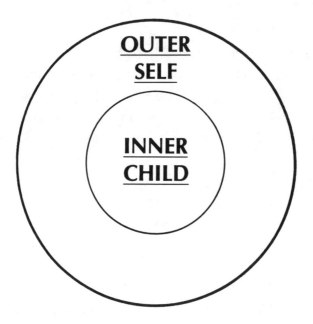

The Inner Child

Think of this inner child as your core being—who you were before you took on all your lifetime roles (son or daughter, husband or wife, mother or father, career person). At birth, you are totally inner child.

Some typical characteristics of this inner child are innocent, playful, creative, spontaneous, honest, and naive. Thus, the picture we get is of a very vulnerable being that needs nurturance and protection from the harsh world. That's what our outer self does.

The Outer Self

The outer self is that part of us we present to the world. From birth we start to build this outer self. We learn that if we cry we will be fed or comforted, if we smile we receive back a smile. As we grow, we learn how to behave properly in the world. We learn how to get along with other children, how to properly get our needs met, and how to keep ourselves happy. In essence, this outer self operates as an adult to our inner child.

Most of our interactions with other people are from the outer self—the conscious mind. When we greet each other in church, we are relating from one outer self to another. When we talk with someone in the store or on the street, our outer selves are doing the talking.

Largely through massive influence from our society, we've learned to totally relate and rely on our outer self for survival. In fact that's the reason so many of us are experiencing difficulties nowadays. Society teaches us through the media to use this or that product to make our outer self look or feel better at the total exclusion of our inner child. And it's exactly these subtle messages that keep our inner child feeling neglected.

As an example, let's picture a typical parent and child on a trip to the grocery store. To make this really graphic, let's say the child is a two-year-old. The adult pushes the shopping cart down the aisles, filling the basket with the needed items. Suddenly the child sees a candy bar.

"I want that," she says.

"No, not now. You can't have it," Mommy answers.

"I want candy!" the toddler wails.

"No."

As the child screams and throws a temper tantrum, everyone in the store looks on. The mother starts to feel uncomfortable, maybe she even thinks she's not being a good parent, that she can't control her child. Usually the result is either a spanking, which produces more tears, or the mother carting the child out of the store, leaving behind a partially full shopping cart.

We've all seen or experienced situations like this. The desires of that two-year-old are much like the desires of our inner child: "I want it, I want it now, and I want it free." Uninhibited expression of feeling.

The needs of that parent are the same needs of our outer self: "I can't let the world see this bad child (inner part of me). What would everyone think?"

The result of this inherent conflict is the inner child trying to express itself and the outer self trying to keep the inner child suppressed where it can't be seen or heard. When this conflict gets intense, we end up with the symptoms I talked about in chapter 1.

But how can you tell if you have such a conflict? We all do, it's a fact of our human makeup. To identify the conflict, we have to know the difference between these two very basic parts of ourselves.

The Difference Between Our Outer and Inner Selves

Let's see how well you can tell the difference. Look over the following statements. If you believe it's outer self talking, put "OS" beside the statement. On the other hand, if you think it is an inner child speaking, put "IC" next to the statement.

● ●

1. ____ My family is normal, well-adjusted. We have a happy life.
2. ____ I think it'd be neat to own a red sports car.
3. ____ I can't afford a new car.
4. ____ I felt hurt today when I was teased or joked about.
5. ____ I feel lonely when you don't call me.
6. ____ It's your fault that we have problems.
7. ____ It's very nice to meet you.
8. ____ I'd like the steak dinner, well-done.
9. ____ I love you.
10. ____ I hate you.
11. ____ I'm really feeling depressed today.

● ●

Sally Dansen had lots of trouble deciding what was her inner child speaking versus her outer self in this exercise. Actually we all do. We are so programmed right from birth to be in our outer self that it's difficult to even tell when our inner child is speaking. And to make it even more difficult, our inner child usually doesn't speak in words, it communicates in emotions and thoughts.

Generally, though, if the words are about feelings and emotions (joy, pain, happiness, anger), that's the inner child speaking. If the speech is logical, matter-of-fact, and unemotional, it's the outer self talking, which can be deceiving.

Numbers nine and ten in the above exercise were feeling statements ("I love you" and "I hate you"). Often the outer self expresses one thing while the inner child feels something totally different.

Now this isn't all bad. In fact, it's necessary to relate from the outer self, especially in the business world. The problem occurs when people emphasize their outer self at the total exclusion of their inner self.

It's a well-known fact that sensitive people, those who want to relate from their inner child perspective, have more difficulty working in the business world. The clue, then, is to find a balance between the outer self and the inner child.

A Balance Between Our Outer and Inner Selves

In a healthy individual (if there is such a thing!), the inner child and outer self can coexist. Both unconscious and conscious thought can occupy the mind. It's the equivalent of an adult and child interacting and interrelating. This person is not afraid of expressing emotions, being creative, spontaneous, and honest—even allowing himself or herself to be vulnerable and thus intimate in relationships. He or she is able to screen the inner child desires in order to function in today's world, but also fulfill those desires in appropriate ways.

As any parent knows, this balance is very tricky to maintain. Children must be nurtured and disciplined at the same time. They must learn delayed gratification and empathy for others' feelings. This happens with maturity and time. It is the same with your inner child and outer self. But what happens if there isn't a balance between these two beings?

When the Scales Tip

"Why are you here?" I asked Sally Dansen. "Tell me what's concerning you."

"I don't know. I'm just unhappy and I know I shouldn't be."

"How so?"

"Well, I suppose it's my fears that worry me the most. For some reason I'm intensely afraid of the dark. Just the other day we had that tremendous thunderstorm. You remember, the one that knocked out power all over?"

"Yeah, I sure do. I was in the shower when it happened."

Sally chuckled. "Thank the Lord I wasn't. But all the lights went out and the house went completely dark. I just freaked. Dave had to calm me down while he tried to find a flashlight. I made Britney and Kevin more scared than they should have been. Those kids are everything to me. Now I'm afraid I'll do something to hurt them. That's when I knew I needed help."

Sally Dansen's symptoms, her recurring depression and moodiness, had developed into full-fledged phobias which were crippling her daily functioning. That's what usually happens to a person when the inner child has been hurt and the outer self tries to keep that hurt hidden behind a facade of normalcy.

Such was the case with Phil Sanderling.

"There was nothing wrong with my childhood that I can recall," he said one day. "Mom and Dad were both good parents. But now I've got this fear of relationships and that's what's bugging me, not my upbringing."

I suspected there was something in Phil's childhood that caused his relationships problems today, but Phil was relating to me from his outer self. If I was ever going to find out what the problem was inside Phil, I had to hear from Phil's inner child.

Getting to the Inner Child

Usually a patient will start to relate to me from the facade of his or her outer self. I might hear small, polite talk about what he or she did that day. Most of my clients begin talking about their lives in a very unemotional, logical tone of voice. However, to make any progress, I have to get through the outer self to the inner child.

The best way to get down to the inner child is to express feelings. That's what I do with my patients. Let's make an attempt to get in touch with your feelings at this point by writing them down. Take a look at Sally Dansen's feelings, as she wrote them, to get an idea of what I'm asking you to do.

> "I feel really unsure about this. I don't know if I want to
> continue. I'm confused, uncomfortable, and scared."

Her last feeling *scared* showed she was slowly getting to her inner child. Something inside her was frightening.

How about you?

> "I feel _____
> _____
> _____
> _____."

Don't worry if you can't think of any feelings or if you're just feeling confused. Write what comes to mind first.

When I hear emotions like fear, I want to cheer. My patient and I are making progress, we're getting down to the core—the inner child.

This is why patients tend to quit treatment at this point. As they start to find their inner child, they experience a whole range of emotions, from joy and ecstasy right down to sorrow and anger. That's why you might be feeling much worse now than when you began this book. This is normal.

If you are feeling doubt and fear right now, go back and read the commitment you signed in chapter 1. Let it empower you to continue. I know it's hard to believe, but the suffering and pain will go away. If you stick with it, they'll go away for good.

Before we go further, we need to take a reading on how comfortable you are expressing emotions. You will not make any headway until you can recognize and articulate these important components of yourself.

Can You Express Your Feelings?

Some of us are better at this than others. If we had a family system in which we weren't encouraged to say how we feel, then we are more likely to keep our emotions to ourselves.

What were your family's rules on expressing emotion? Phil Sanderling, for instance, was taught to suppress his emotions. His father invoked the typical macho male image and taught Phil never to cry or show affection. Thus, it was extra difficult for Phil to write about and talk about his feelings.

Look over the following statements. Check those that apply to your family life as you remember it.

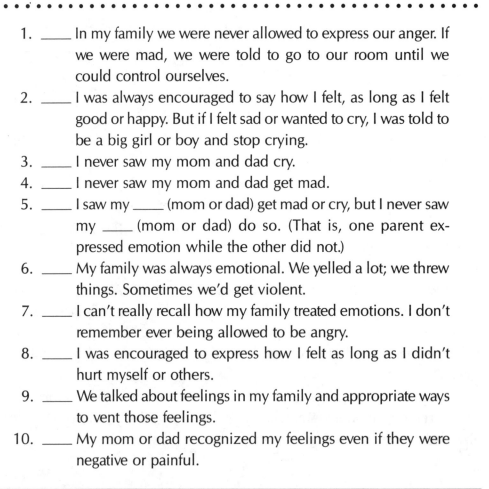

1. _____ In my family we were never allowed to express our anger. If we were mad, we were told to go to our room until we could control ourselves.
2. _____ I was always encouraged to say how I felt, as long as I felt good or happy. But if I felt sad or wanted to cry, I was told to be a big girl or boy and stop crying.
3. _____ I never saw my mom and dad cry.
4. _____ I never saw my mom and dad get mad.
5. _____ I saw my _____ (mom or dad) get mad or cry, but I never saw my _____ (mom or dad) do so. (That is, one parent expressed emotion while the other did not.)
6. _____ My family was always emotional. We yelled a lot; we threw things. Sometimes we'd get violent.
7. _____ I can't really recall how my family treated emotions. I don't remember ever being allowed to be angry.
8. _____ I was encouraged to express how I felt as long as I didn't hurt myself or others.
9. _____ We talked about feelings in my family and appropriate ways to vent those feelings.
10. _____ My mom or dad recognized my feelings even if they were negative or painful.

11. ____ My mom and/or dad freely expressed their feelings and
       dealt with them in an appropriate manner.

• •

If you could check at least one of the first seven statements, you may not be comfortable expressing your emotions as an adult. However, if you could check any of the last four statements, your family may have encouraged you to say how you felt.

Who's to Blame?

The answer to this question is no one. Right from the start I want to assure you I am not here to blame your parents for any wrongdoings in your childhood. The last thing you need to do is become angry and resentful toward your parents.

My purpose is, on the other hand, to try and understand why we act and behave a certain way in adulthood. Our upbringing has a direct bearing on that.

For a moment, visualize yourself as a tape recorder. The tapes that play in this tape recorder are those that were recorded when you were growing up. Suppose something happens that makes you mad. The response you will give is going to be based on the anger tape made when you were growing up. That tape will determine if you might yell or scream or strike out, or if you suppress your anger and act like nothing is wrong.

You might be thinking now, "Oh swell. I'm just one big machine with no capacity to change what's programmed in me."

Well, yes and no. You're obviously not a machine. None of us are. You are like no one else on this earth—completely individual and unique. So you do have the opportunity to change the tapes. However, it's much more difficult than you might think, especially under stress. When a situation is particularly volatile, heated, and emotional, we will revert back to what we learned in childhood.

The main way to stop any detrimental tapes from replaying is to understand what the tapes are. (Remember there are also positive childhood tapes, of joy and love, that we want to keep.)

What Are Your Tapes?

We operate on many tapes as varied as the emotions we feel. Obviously we can't explore all of them within the scope of this book, so I'll just focus on two major ones. The first is anger. Look over the following statements and check those that apply to your situation.

• •

ANGER TAPE

1. When I'm mad, I show it by:
   _____ throwing things
   _____ leaving the room
   _____ hitting something or someone (includes spanking in anger)
   _____ raising my voice
   _____ not saying anything
   _____ pouting/sulking
   other: _____
   _____

2. When either of my parents was mad, they'd show it by:
   _____ throwing things
   _____ leaving the room
   _____ hitting something or someone (includes spanking in anger)
   _____ raising their voice
   _____ not saying anything
   _____ pouting/sulking
   other: _____
   _____

3. When my husband or wife gets mad, he/she shows it by:
   _____ throwing things
   _____ leaving the room
   _____ hitting something or someone (includes spanking in anger)
   _____ raising their voice

_____ not saying anything
_____ pouting/sulking
other: _____
_____

4. When my kids get mad, they:
_____ throw something
_____ leave the room
_____ hit something or someone
_____ raise their voice(s)
_____ are quiet and ignore it
_____ pout/sulk
other: _____
_____

• •

Can you see any pattern to your answers? Look closely at the items that were the same between yourself, your parents, and your children. You learned these tapes as a child and might be passing those tapes on to your children. Now look at your response for your spouse. Is it very different from your own?

If two people are operating on vastly different tapes, they may have problems expressing their emotions to each other. It might be beneficial to have your spouse do just this portion of the workbook so you will have an idea what tapes she or he is operating on.

Now check the following statements to see what tape you operate on when showing happiness and joy.

• •

JOY TAPE

1. When I'm happy, I show it by:
_____ smiling and laughing
_____ talking about it
_____ being excited and enthusiastic

_____ feeling guilty for being happy or waiting for things to get worse

_____ not saying anything. I only talk about my feelings when something's wrong.

other: _____

_____

2. Whenever my parents were happy, they'd show it by:

_____ smiling and laughing

_____ talking about it

_____ being excited and enthusiastic

_____ acting guilty to be so happy

_____ I never remember them acting happy. They only showed anger or sorrow, not joy.

other: _____

_____

3. When my husband or wife is happy, he/she shows it by:

_____ smiling and laughing

_____ talking about it

_____ being excited and enthusiastic

_____ acting guilty to be so happy

_____ not talking about feelings unless something's wrong

other: _____

_____

4. Whenever my kids are happy, they show it by:

_____ smiling and laughing

_____ talking about it

_____ being excited and enthusiastic

_____ acting guilty to be so happy

_____ acting like nothing has happened

other: _____

_____

• •

Again look for the patterns and discern what tapes you and your spouse and your kids are operating on. If you see any disturbing trends, talk about these with someone from your support list in chapter 1.

It is possible to alter our tapes. One of the best ways is to understand when a tape is playing and to see if the tape is valid for the situation.

For example, one of Phil Sanderling's tapes prevented him from showing affection. Through therapy, he understood this was childhood conditioning from his father. Once he knew this, the next time he was afraid to hold Gina's hand in public, he knew it was a holdover from his childhood and not related to the present situation. In essence, it freed his inner child from his outer self.

Understanding why you cover up your inner child with your outer self is at the bottom of all this. Some of it comes from how you were taught as a child. And even more alarming, what you're doing right now, if you're a parent, determines how your children feel about their inner child.

Is the Inner Child Loved by God?

Sometimes patients will say to me "That's too New Age. Christ doesn't want me to mess with the unconscious mind."

While it's difficult to find Scriptures that speak directly of the unconscious mind, there are many passages that speak of wisdom and of the heart. The heart, in biblical times, was considered the human emotional and intellectual center—in essence, our mind.

Proverbs 4:23 says: "Keep your heart with all diligence, for out of it spring the issues of life."

There's nothing about our being that God doesn't know. He created all of our mind, both conscious and unconscious thought. Our inner child is part of His creation.

I firmly believe God directs my Inner Child therapy through the Holy Spirit. In fact, I incorporate prayer as an integral part of my treatment program. Phil Sanderling's prayer at this point read something like the following:

Dear Lord God in Heaven,

I trust in Your faith and guidance. Please help me. Give me strength and wisdom. Don't let me give up when things get tough. Help allay my doubts and fears. And if, at anytime, I'm doing something not good in Your eyes, please give me the conviction and vision to get back on track. More than ever, Lord, I need Your support as I learn about my inner child.

In the Name of Christ Jesus, our Lord,
Phil

Now write your own prayer to God.

Dear God,

_____

_____

_____

_____

_____

_____

_____

_____

_____

Some of my patients say that constant prayer has helped them stick with this program and complete it with long-lasting results.

Right now, make a commitment to have God and Jesus Christ as partners in your inner child exploration.

I, _____, ask God to stand by my side and empower me, by His Holy Spirit, to be strong and convicted to carry out the exercises in this workbook.

3

Step Two

Meeting Your Outer Self and Inner Child

When I have my patients meet these two parts of themselves, I find that using the imagination can be very effective. Likewise in this chapter, I will have you do some exercises with your imagination to get in touch with your outer self and inner child.

Your Outer Self

As I mentioned before, your outer self is who you project to the world. It's your role as a parent, spouse, child, or career person. Most of us have little problem describing this aspect of ourselves.

Begin this exercise by standing in front of a mirror. Sally Dansen had this to say about herself:

"When I look in the mirror, I see a good wife and mother. I see a thirty-four-year-old woman with long brown hair and green eyes. But I also see a confused person who can't decide whether she's happy or sad."

Now look at yourself in a mirror for about a minute. Describe below what you see.

• •

When I look in the mirror, I see _____

_____

_____

_____

_____

_____

_____

_____

_____

. . . .

To further define your outer self, answer the following questions.

. . . .

How do you act when around strangers and acquaintances? _____

_____

_____

How do you act when around family and close friends?_____

_____

_____

Are your two answers different? _____

Why or why not? _____

_____

_____

. . . .

Sally's answers varied, depending upon whom she was with. With strangers and acquaintances, she was a very calm, polite person, she thought. Her emotions were in check and she didn't show any depression or moodiness. With her family, however, Sally opened up more. She thought she showed herself as an unstable person with frequent shifts from good to bad moods.

It's not unusual for there to be a difference in our behavior with strangers and our behavior with our families. Our behavior with strangers is exhibited in our outer self as layers of protection around our inner child. We are more into our outer selves with strangers, whereas with family, we tend to feel less need for the more formal outer self. When Sally looked in the mirror she saw her outer self, but the inner self was trying to come through as well. "I see a confused person who can't decide whether she's happy or sad," Sally said.

Before we meet the other half of ourselves, our inner child, let's begin composing a picture. Below, I've drawn two circles, one inside the other. In the outer circle, write out all the traits you described about your outer self—your physical makeup, the roles you play in your world today, and how you think others see you.

Sally Dansen's diagram looked like the following:

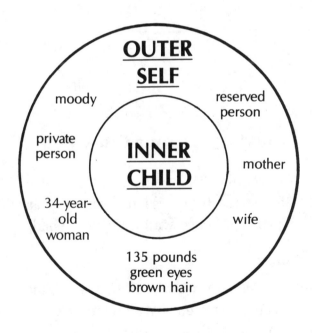

Diagram of Sally Dansen's Outer Self

Now do your own representation of your outer self.

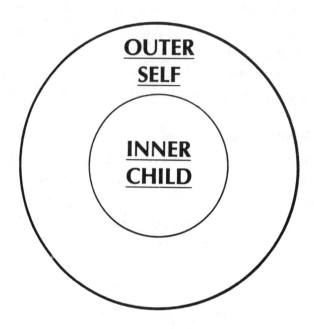

Diagram of My Outer Self

Taking Off Your Outer Self

The following exercises will help you peel off the outer self that covers up your inner child. Perform each exercise in order. They are designed to progressively get you further in touch with your inner child.

1. The Empty Room

My first exercise will have you take off that which makes up your outer self and leave those components outside a pretend room. For this technique, seat yourself in a comfortable chair in a quiet place. Close your eyes and take ten full breaths. When you feel relaxed, picture yourself in front of a room with a door. The door is closed.

Before you can enter the room, you have to remove certain roles that you wear every day of your life. First remove the role of career person (househusband or housewife counts). Next the role as mother or father (if you're a parent). Next your role as a spouse or girlfriend or boyfriend, then your role as a son or daughter. Finally, remove any other roles you play (Scout leader, volunteer fireman, PTA president). In essence, these many components make up your outer self. Leave them on a peg outside the door to this room.

Now enter the room. In the middle of the room you will see a single chair. Sit down in the chair. There's one window in the room, but you can't see through it. While you sit in this chair, think of some of the feelings you are having. When Sally Dansen performed this exercise in my office, she wrote the following feelings: "I feel strange. Not good, not bad. I guess I'd call it numb. I'm not sure this is working. I really don't feel any different than when I walked in Ken's office today."

Now write your feelings below.

• •

I feel _____

_____

_____

_____

_____

_____

_____

_____

• •

If you're not having any emotions or feelings, like Sally, that's fine. Also, if you're experiencing fear or uneasiness, take time now to pray to God and ask the Holy Spirit for comfort and support.

I want you to pretend you are another person looking in from an adjacent room with a one-way mirror. You're looking at yourself seated in the middle of the room. In one of my Inner Child seminars, some of the participants described the being they saw with the following words:

I see a lonely, hurt person;
I see a sad person;
I see an unhappy being;
All I see is an empty chair;
I see a vulnerable, innocent baby.

Describe below what type of person you see.

• •

When I look at me (my inner child) in the chair, I see

_____

_____

_____

_____

_____

• •

If you did see someone and were able to describe that person, you've met your inner child—who you now are inside.

What if you saw only an empty chair or nothing at all or you couldn't describe this being? That's okay. In most cases, people who try this the first time see nothing at all. Or they may describe a stereotype of what they feel a child should be. That's when I try the next exercise.

2. *Childhood Picture*

Find a picture of yourself at the earliest age you remember. If you don't have a picture available, try using the following process, to remember yourself at about age five or six, sitting alone in your room.

• •

Close your eyes and picture the house you lived in when you were this age. Describe it in the following blanks. (Sally's house was a white one-story frame house with a scrubby lawn.) _____

_____

_____

_____

_____

Now picture yourself opening up the front door to this house. What do you see? Describe what the front room looks like, then describe the rest of the rooms. _____

_____

_____

_____

_____

Try to picture your mother. Where is she? What is she doing? (Sally said, "She's in the kitchen, of course, making dinner.") _____

_____

_____

_____

And your father (if you had one living with you at this age)—where is he, what is he doing? (Sally's father was in the living room, reading the paper in a big easy chair.) _____

_____

_____

_____

Do you have any siblings? Where are they? What are they doing? (Sally's two brothers were out playing in the backyard.)

_____

_____

_____

_____

Now picture your room. (Sally's room was painted pink. She had a white bedspread and matching lace curtains.) What did you look like? _____

_____

_____

_____

_____

• •

Picture yourself sitting on your bed in your room. Sally said she was crying in her room.

"Why?" I asked.

"I don't know," she answered.

"What do you look like?" I asked.

"Well, I have long hair in braids so tight my head hurts," she responded. "I'm wearing a plaid dress, I think. And, I'm hugging my doll."

• •

Describe yourself sitting on your bed in your room at this early age. (What are you doing? How are you feeling?) _____

_____

_____

_____

_____

_____

• •

For the next section, keep this vision in your mind. Paste a real picture of yourself at this early age in the space provided on the opposite page. If you don't have such a snapshot, sketch a picture of yourself at this age, based on what you remember. No one's going to look at this, so don't worry if you're not an artist. Most of us aren't. Even a stick picture will do.

My Picture of Myself as a Child

Now look at this picture intently for about one minute. Sally Dansen was able to see something when she brought in a picture of herself as a child.

"Tell me what you see," I said.

"I see myself standing with my parents on the beach," she answered matter-of-factly.

"How do you feel about yourself at this age?" I asked.

"I don't really have much feeling about myself. I don't think I'm happy. See, I'm not even smiling. I don't really like myself here. I was bad a lot and did wrong things."

Sally's response is not that unusual. Many of us whose inner child has been hurt in early childhood will not feel good about that inner child as an adult. (If that's what you feel, don't worry. I'll talk about this further in the next chapter.)

In the blanks below, put down the first feelings and thoughts that come to mind as you look at your picture. How do you feel about the person in the picture? What's he or she like?

• •

When I look at a picture of me as a child, I see _____

_____

_____

_____

• •

Look again at the picture or visualize the being in the chair. Fill in the following statements.

• •

When I see me in the chair, I want to _____

_____

_____

_____

_____

When I look at myself as a child in the picture, I want to _____

_____

_____

Is this child happy? _____

Why or why not? _____

_____

_____

_____

Do you like this child? _____

Why or why not? _____

_____

_____

How do you feel as you look at the picture or visualize your inner child in the chair? _____

_____

_____

• •

If you're still having difficulty coming up with a mental picture of yourself as a child, or you would like a clearer image of yourself, you can try another method.

3. *Transfer Your Childhood Memories*

• •

Think of a child, any child, you know who is about five or six. Describe that child, physically and emotionally.

_____

_____

_____

Now pretend you're switching places with this child, describe him or her now. What does he or she look like, again physically and emotionally?

_____

_____

_____

_____

Go back and draw a rough sketch of yourself as this child in the space to the right on page 43.

How do you feel about yourself as this child? Do you like him or her?

_____

_____

_____

_____

• •

Frequently I hear that my clients don't really like the child they see.

"Why don't you like him?" I asked Phil Sanderling.

"Well, he messes up. He's always getting into trouble. He wants his own way all the time. He's a bother," Phil answered.

"Do you have any nieces or nephews?"

"Sure I do," Phil grinned. "Angela, she's about six, I think."

"Does Angela make mistakes and get into trouble?"

"Well sure, she's a kid. Kids get into trouble."

"So it's okay for Angela to mess up, but not for your inner child, is that right?"

"Well, yeah, I guess. I'm older, I shouldn't mess up or make mistakes," Phil answered.

"You have a different set of standards for yourself than for your niece?"

Phil didn't see this at first. After several sessions, though, he learned that he could allow himself the same latitude to make mistakes as he did his niece. Phil's reaction is also not unusual. Those of us who had a childhood where we were chastised for making mistakes will feel this way about our inner child.

4. *First Childhood Memory*

If you've still had problems visualizing yourself as a child or seeing your inner child in the chair, try and think of a childhood memory—something that happened that you remember when you were five or thereabouts. Maybe it was a family vacation, a picnic, or family outing. Perhaps it's when a sister or brother was born. Whatever event comes to mind, hold on to that memory and then describe the child you were during this event.

- -

When I remember _____ (vacation, birth of a sibling, starting kindergarten), I can describe myself as _____

_____

_____

_____

- -

Draw a rough sketch of yourself at this age in the space below.

• •

How do you feel about the child you were at this time? _____

_____

_____

_____

• •

At this point, you should have a fairly clear picture of who your inner child is and how you feel about this being. Let's make this visual.

Completing the Diagram

Flip back to the diagram you filled in at the beginning of this chapter. In the inner circle, write all the things you can describe about yourself at this early age. Record more than just physical traits; record the emotions you, as a child, were feeling at this point in your life.

Sally Dansen's completed diagram looked like this:

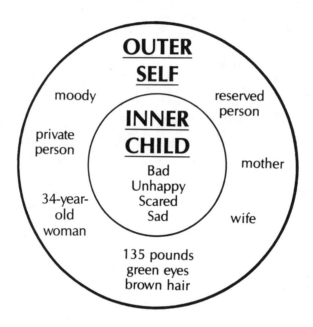

Sally Dansen's Completed Diagram

• •

Look at your inner circle. Do you like yourself at this age? ____ yes
____ no. Why or why not? _____

_____

_____

• •

This exercise can bring up some unhappy childhood memories, especially if you've experienced some sort of trauma at this age.

Sally Dansen started having nightmares at about this point in her therapy. When she described her dreams, I became alerted that she may have
suffered some sort of abuse in her childhood. When she began realizing this
truth, Sally's emotions took a downward spiral. She started feeling distraught.
I obviously began monitoring her progress closely.

Likewise if, through meeting your inner child, you've started having desperate thoughts, please seek help from someone on your support list or contact a professional psychotherapist.

When Sally was ready, I asked her to do another exercise.

"This unhappy little girl you've described to me is still living within you now as an adult; you haven't left her behind. She's still crying out for help now. And, that's why you're feeling the way you do in the present," I explained.

"So what can I do about it?"

"Well, first we have to acknowledge this little girl's existence. Until now you've ignored her."

"How do I do that?"

"For our next session, I want you to write a letter to this little girl inside. Tell her how you feel about her. Pour every thought and feeling out from your head in this letter. Don't try to reread or rewrite this letter. I'm not interested in your writing style. When we meet again, we'll read it together, okay?"

"I guess," Sally answered.

At our next session, Sally brought in the following letter:

✉

Dear Little Sally,

Why have you come back to haunt me now? My life was just getting better, then you came along and made things much worse. I've been trying to get away from you all my life, trying to live a normal life. But you've always been around to mess things up, just as you did at six. If you hadn't been so bad, these things would never have happened. Why don't you just go away? I'm an adult now. I don't need you. And I don't like you.

Sally

I wasn't too surprised to read such a negative letter. Especially in cases of childhood abuse, the patient feels ambivalent or negative toward his or her inner child. *Why else would the abuse have happened to me? I must have been bad to cause it,* is the thought process.

Acknowledging Your Inner Child

Just as Sally Dansen did, so I am asking you to write your inner child a letter. Look at the childhood picture you pasted in or sketched. Or, visualize the being in the chair. Now write a letter to that person. Tell him or her whatever first comes to mind.

Dear _____,

_____

_____

_____

_____

_____

_____

_____

_____

_____

_____

Sincerely,

_____

At about this stage, Sally Dansen's depression became more pronounced. In fact she'd reached the point of feeling much, much worse than when she had begun therapy. You may not be feeling worse. Everyone feels different. If you're not, continue with the book. If you *do* feel much worse than when you started this book, don't fear. Take a moment and pray with me to God for help and comfort:

✉

Dear Lord,

Help me now. Thoughts and feelings are flowing through my head that I can't deal with. I'm really afraid and I need Your shoulder more than ever. Give me the strength and stamina to continue.

As you may endure feelings of pain and suffering through your recovery, think of the suffering our Lord Jesus Christ endured for our benefit. Think of how He persevered against many tribulations and assaults, all for our benefit. When we care enough about ourselves and our relationship with God to persevere, God helps us in our journey through His Holy Spirit.

And not only that, but we also glory in tribulations, knowing that tribulation produces perseverance; and perseverance, character; and character, hope. Now hope does not disappoint, because the love of God has been poured out in our hearts by the Holy Spirit who was given to us. (Rom. 5:3–5)

Again, if your feelings are interfering with your daily functioning, or if you feel like hurting yourself or someone else, contact a professional counselor or psychiatrist.

Feelings

I've attempted to open up some of your inner feelings in this chapter. This is hard for most of us, particularly if we were raised not to show our feelings (as most males were). But if you're to make any further progress, it's important that you start expressing your emotions.

If someone hurts your feelings, acknowledge the hurt (not necessarily to them but to yourself). If someone made you angry, acknowledge your anger. If you feel sad or disappointed, allow yourself to feel that too.

One of the best ways to do this is to begin a daily *Feelings Log*. Write out your feelings every day in a journal or diary.

Your daily log could look like this.

FEELINGS LOG

Tuesday, March 14, 1992:

Today, my boss got mad at me because there was a mistake in the contract I drafted. His comments made me feel angry and hurt.

Even after you've completed this workbook, continue to record your feelings in this daily log. You'll feel better, you'll understand yourself better and, as I'll show you, you'll be acknowledging your inner child.

I recall the first time I acknowledged my feelings as an adult, long ago when I played bass guitar in a country-western band. We musicians are a strange lot.

I was playing with this band in a club one night. During one of our numbers, I couldn't hear myself singing through the monitors. I kept motioning to the sound man to turn my voice mike up, but he refused. After our gig, I asked him why he didn't turn up the volume on my mike.

His reply was, "You're not the main singer, just the bass player. The others are the stars."

Well, I went home and told my wife, Mary Jo, what happened. And I spent most of the next day trying to understand why this guy had said that. Had I done something to him? Was it something I said? I just couldn't understand why he'd acted that way. Mary Jo finally told me why I was consumed with trying to understand the man.

"Your feelings are hurt," she said. "He hurt your feelings."

The more I thought about it, the more I knew Mary Jo was right. I had hurt feelings. It didn't matter why the sound man acted the way he did, I was just hurt.

When we start acknowledging our feelings, we no longer need to search for a reason for another's actions. If you still need a reason for the feelings, it's your outer self trying to rationalize your emotions. And no matter how hard you try, you'll never come up with a rational explanation for emotions.

We need to just allow our inner child to feel. One of the best ways to do this is keeping the *Feelings Log* on a daily basis.

As you start to validate your feelings and allow your inner child to express itself, you will be free from trying to figure out why the world affects you in a certain way. But, as I'll explain in later chapters, allowing yourself to feel the emotions does not mean that you relate to the world on a purely emotional basis. There is still a need for your outer self to project the needs and feelings of the inner child in an adult manner.

What Hurts Your Inner Child?

4

"I can't understand why I'm in this class," Andrew, a participant of one of my Inner Child seminars, said. "I didn't have an unhappy childhood. I was raised in a middle-class family, three-bedroom home in suburbia. So I guess I don't have any injuries to my inner child."

"Well, before you get up and walk out of tonight's session, bear with me a bit," I said. "I know we've discussed some serious abuse cases so far and the reason for this is because they are the best illustrations of this Inner Child concept. But there are many other, less serious ways our inner child can be wounded during childhood. I'm going to cover those types of subtle injuries also."

"Well, what about me?" another participant, Lorna, asked. "I'm having problems at my job."

"And you said your problems were anxiety over job performance, is that correct?" I asked.

"Right. I just can't relate with my boss. He's always critical of my perfor-mance. I'm starting to doubt myself."

I smiled and said, "Let's discuss the basic types of childhood traumas and how those traumas can impact our present-day relationships. If we are to begin validating our inner child, we must first understand the psychological ramifications of any wounds to this being. It's only from this point of under-standing that we can begin healing. It's also only through this process that healthy relationships can exist today, despite what happened yesterday.

"As we begin to discover what hurts your inner child, I want to reiterate that we are not parent-bashing here. All of our parents did the best job they could, given their pasts. It serves no purpose to our recovery or to our families to lay blame. What they did may not have been right, but we don't want to dishonor them.

"Nor do I want to imply that there are healthy family situations and unhealthy ones. In reality there is a continuum between healthy and unhealthy. Most of us fall somewhere in between. What differs is our position on this continuum.

"But, to cover the entire continuum, I have to talk about all the types of injuries an inner child can suffer. Some may apply to you, while others will not. This discussion in its entirety will be useful to everyone, though, because if it doesn't apply to you, the trauma I'm describing just might apply to someone you're involved with either through work, your church, or your family. In this way, the discussion will be important for everyone in the group."

Types of Childhood Trauma

Our inner child can receive two major categories of trauma in early life: abuse and neglect. A whole range of types, which swing from severe, graphic traumas to the very subtle, lies within each of these categories. But all trauma, subtle or graphic, can greatly affect our inner child.

Exactly what makes this possible is the critical boundaries that are violated when a child suffers abuse or neglect. Most of these boundaries center around the child's basic instincts.

When an infant comes into the world, he or she is totally and completely dependent upon the caregiver. This person must provide all the food, clothing, and shelter required for survival. Thus, one of the first developmental tasks of infancy is learning to trust—trust that when the caregiver leaves the room, he or she will return; trust that when the infant needs something, the caregiver will provide it; and trust that the caregiver will provide protection.

This caregiver holds immense power in the eyes of the infant. As this infant grows into childhood, the caregiver and other adults continue to hold power over his or her destiny. These adult figures are the child's first representation of God. In fact, to the child, caregivers and other adults are God. Let's see why.

Think back to your first exposure to spiritual teachings, whether they were in Sunday school, vacation Bible school, or something similar. Phil Sanderling's recollections are similar to what most of us remember from our childhood.

• •

"I remember the punch and cookies in Bible school and the coloring. Jesus was very handsome. I thought he was wonderful. He always had a bunch of kids around Him. All the adults I knew shooed us kids away, but not this guy.

"God, now that's another story. He was a big, big person up in the clouds."

What were your first memories and impressions of God and Jesus?

_____

_____

_____

• •

Basic Concepts Taught to Children About God

1. God is omniscient. He knows everything about everything. ("If you do something wrong, God will know.")
2. God is omnipresent. He is everywhere at all times. "I always wondered how this God could be at the same place all over the world. It just amazed me," Phil commented.
3. God is omnibenevolent. God is always good. He is not capable of doing any evil.
4. God is omnipotent. He is all powerful. There is no one and nothing more powerful than God. (This can be scary stuff for a child, and at the least, humbling for an adult.)

A young child sees these same characteristics in his or her own caregivers.

"Did Daddy or God create the world in seven days?" asked a five-year-old. To the child, the caregiver is God.

Now try to conceive what happens to a child when this "God" hurts him or her through abuse or neglect. Suddenly this God-figure is doing something he instinctively feels is wrong. The child's immature mind will funnel through the following thought process when this happens:

a. This God-adult has done something to me that has hurt me.
b. But this God-adult is not capable of doing or being wrong (he/she is omnibenevolent).
c. Therefore, there is only one explanation. I must be the one who is bad. I must be very bad to cause this person to do this to me.

Sexual Abuse

Sexual abuse is probably one of the most damaging traumas a young child can experience because so many critical boundaries are violated. When a child comes into the world and learns trust, he or she also learns to be dependent upon the caregiver for survival and guidance. In addition, this child is born with innate feelings of the proper lines and boundaries, although the exact dimensions of these boundaries are still very fuzzy and need to be rounded out by the parent through example and guidance.

Now when this caregiver, a parent, sexually abuses this child (whether this is fondling or actual intercourse), the child gets a very confused message. On the one hand, this God-parent is doing something to the child that he or she instinctively knows is wrong. (Usually this instinct is buried deep in the child's unconscious.) What is happening to him or her is *not right*. This God-parent is not protecting or nurturing, he or she is harming. And on the other hand, the child will become even more confused because the parent may communicate the abuse as a way to show love: "You're my special girl" or "Let's keep this our special secret, okay?"

The child's mind will try to make sense out of this trauma. Either he or she will repress the event totally or act like it is happening to someone else. Or, the child will try to rationalize the trauma by following the "a,b,c approach" mentioned above. The child will then truly believe that he or she is bad, very bad to have caused this adult to do this.

The trauma seems to be more pronounced if the perpetrator is the child's parent or primary caregiver. However, another adult can still cause these mental and emotional reactions in the child.

Needless to say, the inner child of this child receives some very intense and negative messages.

MESSAGES TO THE INNER CHILD FROM SEXUAL ABUSE

1. I'm bad to the core.
2. I'm dirty. No one who is good or clean would want to have anything to do with me.
3. My sexuality is bad. After all, if I hadn't been female, the sexual abuse wouldn't have happened.
4. God is disgusted with me.
5. God must think I'm bad also because He didn't protect me.

Where Is God?

The last message is a real humdinger. So many of my patients ask, "Where was God when all this was happening to me?" If I knew the answer, I'd be able to save the world.

It's very hard for us to understand God's position on this, much like a child cannot even conceive why a parent does one thing or another. But let me try to explain it with an illustration from my past.

One afternoon, I was at a lake swimming and fishing with my daughter and her friend. The two girls were swimming when I noticed a cottonmouth snake just offshore from the girls. You can imagine the terror I felt for my daughter and her friend.

"Girls, you've got to swim on in now," I yelled, trying to act calm.

"How come, Daddy? We're having fun."

"Come out of the water, right now."

"But, why!"

"Get out of the water! You heard me!"

"Okay, okay." The two girls started swimming toward shore. I nervously watched the snake.

When they reached shore and climbed up on the bank, my daughter asked, "How come we had to get out?"

That's when I pointed out the snake. If I had told them about the snake while they were still in the water, the girls would probably have panicked and one might have been bitten.

Now, if my daughter had not seen the snake, she wouldn't have understood my actions. Because we cannot see the whole picture as God does, we cannot always understand His intervention on our behalf.

I believe God acts as our perfect parent, protecting us from evil in some ways, but maybe not in the ways we think He should. For our emotional protection as children, God allows us certain defense mechanisms like denial and repression (forgetting an event).

But as we become adults, God slowly takes away those defense mechanisms, and strengthens us to deal with the pain of our inner child. The defense mechanisms serve their purpose well for protecting the fragile inner child being. But as adults, the defense mechanisms can get in our way.

It's the same for a child learning how to ride a bicycle. At first the training wheels are needed to help with balance. But as the child learns how to balance on his or her own, the training wheels get in the way, actually making it even harder to balance on the bike.

These defense mechanisms, like training wheels, work for a period and then lose their usefulness and actually hamper our progress. Thus, I believe that it is in God's plan to remove our defense mechanisms so we can face any childhood trauma and receive healing for our inner child. As we cleanse ourselves of pain, we are more open to God's message in our lives.

Reactions to Sexual Abuse

The inherent feeling of badness from sexual abuse that a child feels serves the perpetrator well. In fact this will be the mechanism to keep a child from telling. Let's look at how this worked in Sally Dansen's childhood.

You'll recall that Sally started having nightmares as she and I progressed with her Inner Child therapy. In her dreams, she was in a darkened room and sensed the presence of someone else. She could barely make out the dim silhouette of a large person. Each time she would wake up screaming.

When I asked Sally if she had been sexually abused, all her childhood memories and trauma came out along with a flood of tears. For a period of several months, while her uncle lived at her house, he repeatedly came into her room and sexually abused her after her parents were asleep. She never told anyone because her uncle said she'd cause her parents to argue and divorce.

Apparently, she and her brothers were frequently left alone with her uncle when her parents went out. Even though she begged them not to leave her, they thought she was being silly and ignored her pleas. The abuse stopped when the uncle moved to another state.

The trauma to Sally's inner child is obvious from this account. Her defense mechanism was to repress the event deep within her unconscious, something that is common when a child is repeatedly abused. The inner child can't accept the message of "badness" so the child represses it (she loses the memory of it). However, this repression often weakens as the child ages. The inner child pain starts to surface, causing all sorts of secondary symptoms and problems. Hence Sally's compulsions and phobias.

I'm definitely not saying that if you have the compulsions or symptoms I mentioned in chapter 1, you've been sexually abused. But you may have had some other more subtle injury as a child, which I'll discuss later.

For now, though, think about how you feel about what you've read. If a person has experienced sexual abuse as a child and is aware of it, he or she will commonly feel one of two very distinct feelings after reading this section. This story may invoke intense feelings of pain and sadness. Or the person may feel detached, as if the trauma happened to someone else. Both reactions are natural.

Sally felt distraught, emotional, and desperate. Her reaction was the first I described above. She even battled with suicidal thoughts off and on throughout this period in her therapy.

Fill in the following blanks with your feelings.

. . . .

I feel _____

_____

_____

_____

. . . .

Again, if you're having desperate thoughts (thinking about suicide) and/or experiencing self-destructive behaviors (such as substance abuse), please seek help from your support people or a professional counselor.

Effects of the Inner Child Messages from Sexual Abuse

Basically, as the defense mechanisms begin to weaken, the adult may experience problems primarily with relationships with others. Four major relationship problems may surface:

1. Fear of the perpetrator

If the victim still has contact with the perpetrator, he or she will feel afraid and intimidated in the perpetrator's presence. Indeed, whatever self-esteem and healing the victim has been able to do may vanish in the presence of this person. That's why I don't recommend that my patients confront the perpetrators once they realize what happened.

2. Displaced anger

Sexual abuse victims typically displace their feelings to others around them. If the trauma caused by the abuse has not been healed, the victim may be angry with others who weren't even directly involved—perhaps the other parent who didn't protect the child, or God. Even more common is anger toward all people of that gender. It's safer for the victim to be mad at all people of the perpetrator's gender than to face the event and be angry with a specific perpetrator. I know I'm making real progress when my patients finally get angry at their perpetrators.

3. Denial of gender

Often a victim will be very uncomfortable with his or her own gender. Females who have been abused by males may not be comfortable being feminine. They may wear masculine clothes and take on masculine mannerisms. Deep in their unconscious, women who have been abused may mistakenly blame their femininity as the cause.

4. Fear of intimacy

Another relationship problem that stems from childhood sexual abuse is failure to establish an intimate relationship with another human being. Obviously sexual abuse victims do meet and marry in adulthood; however, they typically never get really close to their mates.

To be intimate, you have to be willing to open yourself up and be vulnerable. Of course, victims are afraid to open up; they've been hurt before. And if they did open up, what would that other person think of them? Remember the very strong inner-child message since childhood has been, "I am bad, dirty to the core." Therefore, if this person allows another to see his or her inner child, they will see how bad and dirty he or she is.

Thus, victims live in constant fear that others will find out how bad they really are and leave them. So victims of childhood sexual abuse tend to be very guarded in their relationships, operating constantly from the outer-self perspective. They can appear warm, pleasing, polite, interesting to talk to, but deep inside, they are actually frightened little children. Interestingly, this can occur even if the abuse memory remains repressed.

The Effort of Mining

When I start to work through the childhood memories of abuse with my patients, the going gets rough and tough. Sally Dansen felt like quitting her Inner Child therapy at about this time. "I feel terrible. I can't go through the day without breaking down into tears. Dave wonders what is wrong. Instead of getting better, I'm getting worse," she told me.

I got her permission to call Dave and explain what was happening. "Dave,

Sally is going to really need your help. She's recently gotten in touch with a traumatic period in her childhood," I explained.

"I know. She told me all about it. I just can't believe it. But I guess now that I know, it sort of ties a lot of loose ends together," Dave answered.

"What sort of loose ends?" I asked.

"Well, nothing in particular, just Sally's behavior toward men, including me, at times. And her actions toward her parents, especially her dad."

"Exactly. Well, she's going to be very emotional until we resolve and heal this deep hurt inside her. I'm asking for your support. Let her know you love her no matter what and that you'll stand beside her all the way. Just saying those words will mean a lot to Sally."

If you are feeling uneasy at this point, I again advise you to call someone on your support list or a professional counselor. Just knowing someone is there for you will give you the courage to go on. At this point, I also recommend prayer.

Remember how much our Lord Jesus Christ suffered for our well-being. God will not forsake you as you continue your quest: "And the Lord, He is the one who goes before you. He will be with you, He will not leave you nor forsake you; do not fear nor be dismayed" (Deut. 31:8).

To encourage patients like Sally Dansen to stick with it, I remind them that Inner Child work is not unlike striking it rich in a gold mine.

In most underground gold mines, there are several passageways; new ones are dug deeper into the mountain to follow the gold vein. If we look at Inner Child work as one would look at a gold mine, we see that we have several passageways to go through before we reach the gold vein.

Each passageway runs progressively deeper into the mountain. It takes lots of work to go through the deeper passages. And it especially takes lots of work to dig out the gold once the vein is located.

If you picture your discovery of your inner child as a gold mine, you start out about midway in the mine at the shaft hole. Here you may be experiencing some emotional problems such as depression or anxiety. As you go deeper into the mine of this workbook, you may come up against some compulsions or symptoms (such as perfectionism, substance abuse, or phobias). You slowly unveil these compulsions and symptoms until you come up against your last layer—denial and/or repression. It takes lots of work to pick through this last layer; you might even need dynamite.

Finally, however, you break through. The tunnel is darker on the other side. You might fear a cave-in or landslide as the pain and suffering worsen. However, you're not alone in this gold mine. God is there, leading you by a rope. His headlamp (the Holy Spirit) is illuminating the way.

Just when you think you can't go any further, there it is! The gold vein is far at the end of a tunnel, waiting for you, sparkling in God's and your headlamps.

After you find the gold and dig it out, you put it in an ore car and travel back up a different passageway to a new portal at the top. You come out of the mine much richer than you were when you went in.

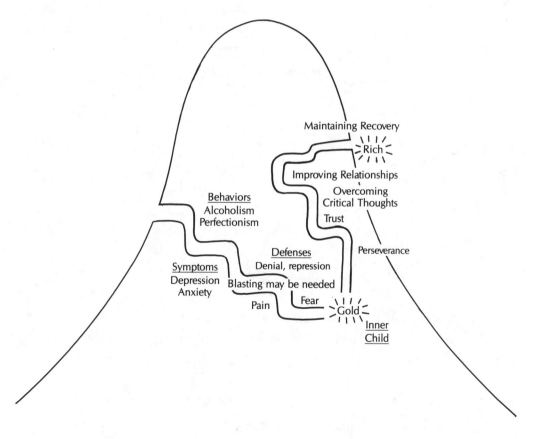

The Gold Mine of the Inner Child

It takes some special tools to get to the gold—a pick, jackhammer, and shovel. Our tools to get to our inner child are the exercises in this book.

Now fill in your own special gold mine. When you come to the inner child—your gold vein, circle it and label it "riches."

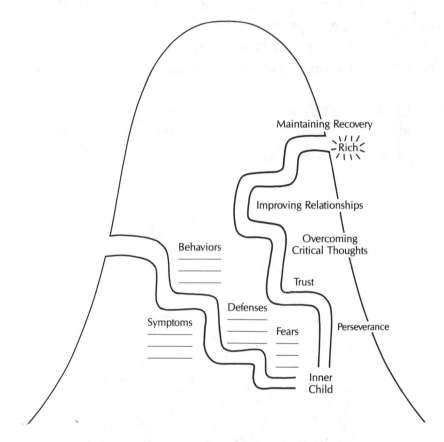

The Special Gold Mine of Your Inner Child

Before we go further into this gold mine, you need to reaffirm your commitment to the process. How open are you to continuing? Check which of the following statements applies to you.

• •

_____ I'm shocked to learn about all the things that are hidden inside me.

_____ I'm afraid of my feelings and I'm holding them back.

_____ I'm committed to continue. I want to discover more about my
       inner child.

Do you have any overriding anxieties or fears about continuing at this
point? If so, what are they? _____

_____

_____

Are you afraid of the pain and suffering you might have to re-
experience? Are you unsure whether you have the strength and deter-
mination to continue? _____ yes _____ no

       What have you accomplished so far in this workbook that you
are proud of? _____

_____

_____

What haven't you accomplished or avoided in these exercises? _____

_____

_____

What are you hoping to accomplish in the rest of this workbook?

_____

_____

_____

Physical and Spiritual Abuse

5

Sheila Cronkhite was a client of mine. She came to me for help because of her husband, Wayne's, behavior. He was out of work. Along with his unemployment compensation, she was supporting the family on her meager salary as a salesclerk.

"I need to get Wayne into counseling," she told me. "We're about broke. He drinks away most of our income. I can't buy new clothes for the kids, Dwayne and Sandy. I've had to sell off some of my jewelry and furniture just to buy shoes for them."

"Tell me a little bit about your relationship with your husband," I said.

"Well, I love him of course. It's just when he drinks that things get rough. I have to shut the kids away in a room. He hits me some, but never the kids. And he's always sorry later."

Many of us wonder why women like Sheila stay with such abusive husbands. There's usually a wounded inner child at the root of this.

Physical Abuse

There are two main types of physical abuse: abuse with anger and abuse without anger. The first is the most common, but the latter also occurs in our society.

Abuse with Anger

This abuse involves the presence of intense, uncontrolled anger directed at the child. Often the anger comes on without any provocation; the child may not even see it coming.

A childhood characterized by anger-generated physical abuse usually results in a perception of anger as an emotion that is bad and must be avoided at all costs. It's an emotion to fear and watch out for. Children who grow up in abusive homes become experts in what I call "environmental scanning." They are constantly checking the volatility of a situation to see if it is safe.

Before we go on, think back to how the family you grew up in treated anger. Sheila grew up in a home where her mother and father did not appropriately deal with their anger, particularly her mother. Sheila had three younger siblings all within five years of her. Needless to say, her mother was saddled with major child-rearing responsibilities. This was further compounded because Sheila's father left the family every winter to earn a living as a fisherman off the coast of Alaska. Sheila could answer "true" to at least three of the following statements.

How about you? Answer the following questions true or false.

. . . .

_____ In my family, we were never allowed to show our anger.

_____ I can't remember ever seeing my dad mad.

_____ I can't remember ever seeing my mom mad.

_____ Boy, when my dad got mad, I had to really watch out.

_____ When my mom got mad, she yelled at or hit us kids.

_____ I frequently got spanked when either my dad or my mom was really mad.

_____ I got spanked if I showed my anger.

_____ Hitting was a frequent form of punishment in my family.

_____ When I got mad, my parents told me to go to my room.

_____ I really can't remember what my parents taught me to do when I got angry.

. . . .

If you could answer even one of the above statements "true," you may not have received a positive education on anger management as a child. Now look over the following statements, check those that apply to you.

• •

_____ I only got spanked after my mom or dad had cooled off.

_____ My parents allowed me to be angry and taught me to channel that anger appropriately so as not to harm myself or others.

_____ We talked about anger as a valid emotional feeling in my family.

_____ I rarely saw either of my parents out of control with their anger. My mom or dad would usually leave the room or use some method to cool down before confronting the situation.

• •

Conversely, if you could check one of the above statements you may be one of those who were taught how to deal appropriately with anger.

Now answer the following questions.

• •

When I get angry I _____

_____

_____

When I get angry at my children, I _____

_____

_____

• •

Look closely at your answer to the last question. Do you tend to spank your children when you're angry or do you yell at them? If so, it's something to think about. Even the most ardent supporters of spanking, don't recommend spanking in anger.

How you were taught to deal with your anger in your childhood (either by example or words) will determine to a large degree how you will deal with your anger as an adult and how you will teach your children to deal with their anger.

For example, Sheila grew up seeing her mother fly into uncontrollable rages which sometimes resulted in physical punishment. As we progressed in her therapy and talked about Wayne, I found that Sheila suppressed her own anger. It was there all right, smoldering under the surface, but it had turned into depression—a form of suppressed anger, thus her passive attitude about her husband's abusive behavior.

Anger is an emotion that we should be allowed to feel. It's a very necessary emotion that, if rightly directed, can produce some positive results.

We get into problems when we suppress (ignore) this anger or vent it in physical and/or violent means toward another person. Anger misdirected and channeled as physical abuse to a child can imprint detrimental messages on this child's inner being.

Abuse Without Anger

Abuse without anger involves premeditated, repetitive actions against a child to invoke pain and suffering. Ritualistic abuse associated with satanic cults is an example of this. This type of physical abuse is devastating to a child and causes long-lasting, serious psychological effects. Many victims of ritualistic abuse develop Multiple Personality Disorders or other serious psychological disturbances to cope with the graphic trauma they have experienced. I strongly recommend that if you even suspect this in your past, you seek professional psychological help immediately.

Ritualistic abuse victims commonly feel they are unworthy of God's love because they feel "dirty." They are even ashamed to relate the events to a therapist. I have heard some very painful, graphic accounts of childhood ritualistic abuse. But keep in mind, no memory is too bad for the Lord to hear and heal.

> "I waited patiently for the Lord;
> And He inclined to me,
> And heard my cry.

He also brought me up out of a horrible pit,
Out of the miry clay,
And set my feet upon a rock,
And established my steps."
(Ps. 40:1–3).

Both anger-generated and non-anger-generated physical abuse send very powerful, negative messages to a child.

Inner Child Messages of Physical Abuse

A child trying to sort out why a person is hurting him or her will not have the rationalizing capabilities of an adult. She or he will not be able to say, "Well, Dad's been under a lot of pressure lately and he's just projecting his anger at me."

Young children are not sophisticated enough to make this conclusion. So instead, their inner child will receive one or more of these messages.

1. I'm bad to the core. (Sound familiar? This is the primary message to the inner child from almost all childhood trauma.)
2. Anger is a bad thing. I must never get angry or I'll hurt someone too.
3. The world is a hostile, alien place. People in the world are so unpredictable, I must try extra hard not to get someone mad at me.
4. Love hurts. Grown-ups only hurt you because they love you.

Notice that these messages often seem irrational and confusing. That's exactly what the inner child experiences.

Sheila experienced this confusion as a child. She couldn't see that her mother was stressed trying to raise a family as a single parent. She thought her mother's behavior was normal; to be loved is to be hurt. She also had a very low self-esteem, because of her inner child message: "I'm bad to cause my mother to hurt me. I need this physical punishment to keep me in line."

These inner child messages will spill over into adulthood as the victim tries to make and maintain relationships with others.

1. Repeating History

No matter how irrational it seems, abuse victims will tend to choose mates who are abusers. Sheila Cronkhite did this with her husband. This is partly due to the power of the unconscious mind. Remember her inner child message?

2. Parenting Difficulties

Victims of parental physical abuse typically do not know how to manage their children's behavior because they themselves have not had good parenting models. Thus, victims of physical abuse will experience some difficulty parenting their own children. Either they will tend to repeat the physical abuse on their own children, or they will vow never to hurt their own children as they were hurt. The latter parent will tend to become overprotective and hovering, keeping the children from learning how to become independent.

In no way do I mean to imply that all abuse victims will treat their children in these ways; many have recovered and gone on to be normal, healthy parents. However, the only way they were able to do so was to first recognize their past and overcome these relationship tendencies.

3. Intimacy

Victims of physical abuse, like sexual abuse victims, will have difficulty establishing intimate relationships. Some will expect physical and emotional pain from those who love them. Without working through the issues of physical abuse in therapy, victims may not be able to maintain deep relationships with anyone.

Spiritual Abuse

As part of a Christian counseling clinic, I am well aware of this problem. Spiritual abuse is the act of manipulating or demeaning another person through the use of Scripture. Another way to put it is, "Emotional abuse in the name of God."

Spiritual abuse is particularly hard to treat because it is disguised as pure spirituality, and those who are questioned about their spiritual upbringing become defensive. What's even harder is that most spiritual abusers feel they're doing no wrong. They honestly feel they are doing to the child what God wants them to do.

Spiritual abuse can be subtle or severe and either implied or stated.

Implied Spiritual Abuse

In this type of spiritual abuse, the church and Scriptures are used to punish the child for wrongdoings. Unfortunately this causes these things to be feared by the child. In essence, the child is taught that God is a judgmental and angry God just waiting to catch the child doing something wrong. These things are not stated to the child, but implied by the actions of others.

"Whenever I got in trouble, my dad made me read the Bible for hours on end," Adrienne told me.

Another patient, I'll call Tom, attended a parochial school. If he acted up, he was told to sit, for several hours, under the altar in the large chapel. This form of punishment is really no different from sending a child to a dark closet.

This type of abuse programs people to view themselves and others constantly from a judging position, always watching to see if someone has done something wrong. Unfortunately, implied spiritual abuse is more prevalent than you might think.

Stated Spiritual Abuse

Stated spiritual abuse, on the other hand, is more obvious but no less damaging to the inner child. Certain things are said over and over to a child until they become ingrained into the child's unconscious and conscious mind.

Check those statements that you have heard in some form or another during your childhood.

• •

_____ If you sin, you will go to hell. (The inference here is that there is no chance for forgiveness or repenting.)

_____ God will only love you if you are reading your Bible and going to church. (Meaning, you have to earn His love.)

_____ If you have even one unholy thought, you are possessed by the devil. (This means we are all possessed.)

_____ If you do wrong, God will strike you dead.

_____ You are so bad. God wants nothing to do with you.

• •

If you could check even one of these statements, you have experienced stated spiritual abuse in one form or another.

Messages to the Inner Child from Spiritual Abuse

At this point, you could probably write these out from memory. The first message is the same no matter what the abuse.

1. I'm bad. God could not possibly love me. Therefore no one else can either.
2. Even though I'll try to be good, I'll never succeed because deep down, I'm really bad.

These statements show the very detrimental effect spiritual abuse has on a child. Without recovery, an injured inner child cannot climb back from this pessimistic thinking.

Effects of Spiritual Abuse on Other Relationships

The net effect of spiritual abuse is that the victim feels unworthy of others' love. Sometimes this feeling of inferiority will create self-fulfilling prophecies.

In addition to feelings of inferiority, victims of spiritual abuse will experience problems trusting others, especially those who claim they have the victim's best interest in mind (such as psychotherapists!). These people have never learned to trust God. If you can't trust God, whom can you trust?

Because spiritual abuse victims will try extra hard to do what is right and please others, they will also cling to relationships in a desperate attempt to get validation from others.

These victims will also have a distorted spiritual view of God and the church. They will fear the perpetrator who invoked the spiritual abuse and, on a deeper level, may even feel anger toward this person and God. However, they will likely be afraid to show this anger because it would only reinforce the inner child messages already given. They will be very confused over the difference between God and religion and many times will reject both, as Tom did.

After his parochial school education, Tom left Christianity and became an atheist. It was only after recovering from his spiritual abuse that he was able to comprehend a loving and caring God.

Think a moment about your childhood and your religious upbringing. Again, I am not probing for problems that aren't there. If you can't think of any forms of abuse or neglect in your childhood, don't try to make some up to fill in the blanks of this workbook. Count yourself one of the lucky ones. Many of us aren't.

. . . .

What were your earliest memories or perceptions of church and/or God?

_____

_____

_____

Did you ever fear God? _____ yes _____ no

If yes, what made you afraid of Him? _____

_____

_____

Were you taught that God was a benevolent, loving God with an unlimited potential to forgive your transgressions? _____ yes _____ no

If no, were you taught that God was a fire and brimstone God, just waiting to judge us mortals and punish us for our mistakes? _____ yes _____ no

Do you feel you are
　　　_____ inherently bad
　　　_____ inherently good
　　　_____ neither

• •

This last question also applies to how a child is taught to feel about himself or herself—what we now call self-esteem. Abuse attacks self-esteem because it communicates, "You are bad, very bad, to cause me to hurt you."

In all forms of abuse, the victim may confuse the perpetrator with God. In spiritual abuse, the victim may see the perpetrator as God.

6

Neglect

Robert Benson's father was a career army general. He was absent from the family both physically and emotionally. When he was around, he had very high expectations of Robert. In fact, Robert was rarely allowed to make a mistake without being chastised for it. Robert's father never gave Robert validation and self-confidence. As a result, Robert had to try extra hard throughout his life to win the approval of his father. He eventually carried this over into other relationships. His intense workaholism was an attempt to meet his unreal self-demands as well as trying overly hard to please his boss and co-workers.

He, at first, denied anything wrong had happened in his childhood. We spent several sessions discussing the nature of his workaholism—why he had this overwhelming desire to please everyone around him. Robert tried to see his inner child with my visualization exercises many times, to no avail. Then one day . . .

"Robert, you brought in a picture of yourself as a young boy," I commented. "Can you tell me about yourself at this age?"

"I was a middle child. I was the responsible one. But, I don't remember ever being a typical, happy child. I always tried to get my father to like me. He was very strict, as I've told you."

"I want you to close your eyes and picture yourself at this age sitting in your bedroom. Got that vision?"

"Yeah."

"Good. Now tell me the first feelings that come to mind as you picture yourself at this age."

"I feel disappointed in myself. Today I got an 'A' on my spelling test. When I showed it to my dad, he acted matter-of-fact. 'That's what we expect of you, boy,' was all he said."

Robert, a grown man of forty, broke down into tears in my office. I wanted to hug him. He'd finally done it—broken through his defense layers. His inner child injury had surfaced and now Robert recognized it. Although he was not physically harmed, he had suffered mental and emotional anguish for many years. He really didn't like his inner child very much.

Robert had to be hospitalized for part of his therapy. The feelings and emotions that surfaced from this discovery became too much for him to handle. (While hospitalization isn't always indicated for Inner Child therapy, it was certainly the best option in Robert's case.) Robert's inner child injury was a form of neglect.

Neglect

Neglect is really the opposite of abuse, because instead of doing something to a child, the perpetrator is not doing something. Neglect is when a child's basic needs are not met.

Every human being arrives in the world with basic needs. These needs are both physical and emotional.

Basic Physical Needs
- Food and water
- Protection from the environment
- Care for illnesses and injuries

Basic Emotional Needs
- Love
- Significance
- Acceptance

As a child, these needs have to be fulfilled first by the parents, then by significant other adults, and finally by peers. If a young child has an unmet need, he or she is not sophisticated enough to look elsewhere for the fulfillment of that need. The inner child message from an unfulfilled need is: "I'm not worthy enough to have this need filled, so I must be bad."

Therapists have found that if the parents do not meet a child's needs, another adult can substitute, but he or she will never be Dad or Mom. That's how critical the parental role is.

Most of the problems we experience as adults occur because we have an unmet childhood need. We look throughout our adult lives for ways to fulfill that need.

Let's look at some specific ways neglect can actually manifest.

Emotional Neglect

A child who has not had his or her emotional needs met has probably not been validated, felt loved, or been allowed to make mistakes. The parent who berates a child for making mistakes and not living up to his or her standards implies that the child is unworthy of the parent's love. The same applies to a child who is not criticized but simply ignored.

Robert Benson fell into both of these categories. His father criticized him for making mistakes and discounted good performance. When a child is treated this way, the inner child receives very distinct messages of worthlessness, insignificance, and of being unlovable.

These messages are incorporated into the inner child and can actually become self-perpetuating. The child will grow up feeling inferior to others.

"If people knew who I really was, they wouldn't like me," Robert told me. Since Robert was not validated as a child by either parent and sought his validation from others, he could never allow himself to be intimate with another human being. He threw himself into his job and his church, looking to his roles for self-validation.

Even though these messages were given him early in childhood, they remained. We have the idea that we can say things to our children and they'll forget. They don't forget. Words stay with a child forever, especially hurting words. The outer self might forget, but the inner child remembers.

Negative statements go by the "3 to 1" rule. At least three positive statements are needed to override the effects of only one negative statement. What do you remember when reading a critique of a movie in the paper—the positive comments or the one criticism? The criticism of course. We harp on the negative statements and gloss over the positive.

Positive reinforcement starts way back from the finish line, thus more of these statements are needed to win the race against the negative messages.

Emotional neglect and emotional abuse are similar in this way. Emotional abuse involves stated and purposeful negative messages. Emotional neglect implies them. Both damage and hurt an inner child.

How does emotional neglect happen in a family?

Underinvolved Parents   In a perfectly balanced family, both Mom and Dad are equally involved in parenting. Mom teaches the child sensitivity and compassion while Dad instructs in self-reliance and work. And, hopefully, Dad models sensitivity while Mom models responsibility. The net result should be a child who is capable of feeling for others and himself or herself as well as being responsible.

The opposite sex parent is largely responsible for meeting the emotional needs of the child while the same sex parent is responsible for modeling appropriate behavior. Mom meets son's emotional needs while Dad models appropriate masculine behavior. Dad meets daughter's emotional needs while Mom models appropriate feminine behavior.

What happens when one or both parents fail to do this?

An uninvolved Dad, like Robert Benson's father, has a neglecting effect on both a male and female child. Little girls need validation from Dad to feel comfortable and confident around other men. When Dad is unavailable to his daughter, she doesn't get this validation. She may go to great lengths to get this attention from Dad—becoming a tomboy, for instance, or competing with Mom for Dad's love. What's sad is that if Dad is emotionally unavailable to his daughter, there's a strong chance he's also unavailable to his wife. This only intensifies the competition between daughter and Mom.

Inner child messages to a daughter because of an uninvolved Dad can include:

- I'm not good. If I were, Dad would want me more;
- I have to try extra hard to get Dad to like me;
- Little girls are inferior to little boys, because Dad spends more time with brother than me;
- I have to become a little boy to get Dad to like me.

An uninvolved dad with a male child will not typically have these same emotional effects, since Dad doesn't primarily meet this child's emotional needs. Robert Benson, however, did get some of these internal messages, particularly the first one, "I'm no good."

In addition to these emotional effects, a male child might never learn appropriate male behavior, when Dad is either physically or emotionally absent.

It's interesting to note that Dad being physically absent is not as detrimental as Dad being present but emotionally absent. Somehow, if Dad is home but emotionally unavailable to the children, I believe the children suffer more lasting effects into adulthood.[1]

A son may have difficulty being comfortable as an adult male. He may behave either in a "feminine" manner or in an overly aggressive "masculine" manner, which he perhaps learned at school or from television. Either way, he may have trouble relating to other adult males.

A daughter may be profoundly affected by an emotionally distant father. She may grow up either avoiding all males or having relationships with several male partners, seeking male validation. Both situations tend to produce an approach-avoidance pattern. A woman will become deeply involved with men very quickly and then fearing rejection, will either break off the relationship or cling even tighter. Either way, she may become codependently involved with this other person.[2]

---

[1] For more information on a father's role in the family, I recommend *The Father Book* by Dr. Frank Minirth, Dr. Paul Warren, and Dr. Brian Newman (Nashville: Thomas Nelson Publishers, Inc., 1992).

[2] For more detail on codependent relationships, I highly recommend *Love Is a Choice* by Dr. Robert Hemfelt, Dr. Frank Minirth, and Dr. Paul Meier (Nashville: Thomas Nelson Publishers, Inc., 1989).

When Mom's emotionally absent, it's the son who will emotionally suffer more than the daughter. (In fact, the daughter may be secretly glad Mom's out of the way so she can have Dad all to herself. This even exists in the healthiest of families.)

A male child's need for nurturance and safety will be unfulfilled. He will either react by deciding he doesn't need this, or he will always search for a mother-figure to fulfill his emotional needs. (This also happens when there's an overinvolved Mom.) He may react in both ways, rejecting nurturance on the conscious level and craving it on the unconscious level.

His inner child messages from this neglect are:

- I must find someone to take care of me;
- Sooner or later all females will abandon me;
- I can only relate to women on a childish basis so they will take care of me.

This last message reflects what therapists now call the "Peter Pan Syndrome." The son will forever relate to women as caregivers and turn on the little boy charm to secure this caretaking. This is one aspect of codependency.

Now to make this discussion more interesting, let's imagine that a daughter with an uninvolved father meets a son with an uninvolved mother. Each is looking to the other to fulfill unmet emotional needs. To illustrate what happens in this case, let's look at a mathematical equation:

$$.5 \text{ (girl with unmet needs)} \times .5 \text{ (boy with unmet needs)} = .25$$

Simply, two dependent people together wind up with less than they started with.

What happens if one of these people meets someone without any unmet needs? The resulting equation is:

$$.5 \times 1 = .5$$

This relationship will usually not last, because the person who was not dependent in the beginning (the 1), winds up with less than he or she started with. The independent person will usually leave the dependent person.

That's where Robert Benson was with his marriage. Marilyn, his wife, was probably closer to a 1, fairly independent. Fortunately for their marriage, he entered therapy to try to change his .5 dependence to a 1 independence.

The moral of this mathematical illustration is that God created us unique and whole. You don't need anything or anyone else to make you complete. When two dependent people enter a relationship, each takes from the other and the net result is less wholeness than each had to start with. Only God through recovery can restore our wholeness (our "1") and thereby restore our relationships.

How about you? If you're married or involved with a significant other, what would your equation look like now?

Can you see room for improvement? You can't change someone else, but you can choose to change yourself. And if you change, the relationship will also change.

Overinvolved Parents   We're all familiar with this type of parent. They are the ones who cannot allow their children to assume any responsibility. Mom will grab her toddler just before he falls or will hover over baby's crib to make sure she's still breathing. Dad will get mad at his son's football coach if he's too tough. These parents will fight their children's battles, attempting to protect them from the hostile world.

To make things worse, in most families with an uninvolved parent, there is an overinvolved one trying to take up the slack. What results is a child pulled between two extremes with neither parent modeling appropriate behavior. This is what we call dysfunction.

Children of overinvolved parents receive two very different sets of inner child messages.

The first type of inner child messages include:

- The world is a hostile, alien place out to get me;
- It's not safe to take risks;
- I need someone to take care of me. I'm not capable to care for myself.

The second type of inner child messages include:

- The world owes me. It must provide me what I want, when I want it.
- There are no consequences for my actions. I can do whatever I want and someone else will take the consequences.
- I'm superior to others. Everyone else must cater to my needs.

. . . .

Do any of these statements sound familiar? ____ yes ____ no   If so, which group would you put yourself in? _____

. . . .

Overprotected children seem to fall either in the first group or the second, without logical reason. Those who fall in the first group will live seemingly boring lives—constantly at the same job, in the same routine, doing whatever they can to avoid taking risks and making changes.

Group 2 individuals will be quite the opposite. They will be selfish, narcissistic people who have little compassion for others' feelings. They will make many demands on their mates and will have high expectations for those around them. They will approach relationships as if asking, "What can this person do for me?"

Chapters 4, 5, and 6 have been very abbreviated primers on the types of trauma an inner child can suffer. The overriding message from these injuries is: "I am unworthy or bad."

. . . .

If you found yourself in one of the situations described in these chapters, which one was it? _____

_____

_____

_____

_____

    Do the inner child messages from that trauma sound familiar, like you've heard them before, maybe over and over? _____ yes _____ no

If you did not find yourself in the types of trauma described in chapters 4, 5, or 6, take a moment and expound on what type of childhood you experienced. What were the unhappy times? Why were they unhappy? What made you the most uncomfortable in your family? _____

_____

_____

_____

_____

What are the inner child messages that might be operating within you right now based on your upbringing? _____

_____

_____

_____

How might these messages be affecting your current relationships?

_____

_____

_____

• •

    Again, I want to state: I am not on a "witch hunt" with you for the purpose of punishing your parents or any other adult for hurting your inner child. I don't want to conjure up anything that isn't there. However, there are few of us in the world, myself included, who have not experienced some sort of childhood trauma. If we don't admit the trauma, we repress it. God certainly knows it exists. "And there is no creature hidden from His sight, but all things are naked and open to the eyes of Him to whom we must give account" (Heb. 4:13).

7

Step Three

Embracing Your Inner Child

Continuing on our gold hunt, our helmet headlight shines on a vein at the end of a dimly lit tunnel. There it is! Instant wealth! Here and there, we glimpse a sparkle. Now how do we get the gold out and in our ore car?

We began to meet our inner child in chapter 3, but there were certain traumas that blocked us. We learned about these in the preceding three chapters. Now it's time to embrace and really see the true inner child.

Before we do that, let's take a short self-test to see if you have removed the blockages.

Self-test of Denial

Complete the following statements.

• •

1. I'm afraid that if others see the *real me*, they will

_____

_____

_____

_____

2. I do a good job of pretending to be _____

_____

_____

_____

3. While on the inside I am really _____

_____

_____

_____

• •

If you found that your answers to numbers two and three were the same or very similar, you may still be blocking your true inner child with denial. All of us refrain from showing our true selves to the outside world, but we need to be able to recognize some difference between who we are inside and who we are on the outside.

If you found yourself still denying and not seeing your inner child clearly, go back and redo the exercises in chapter 3. Then return to this point and continue. (If you are still not seeing your inner child clearly after this, just continue. Some people take longer to see their inner self than others, and some can only see it intellectually. That's okay. Either way, progress is being made.)

Phase 1—Acknowledging Your Inner Child

Sally Dansen didn't like her inner child. In fact, her first letter to this being was very negative. Sally even blamed her inner child for the childhood sexual abuse inflicted upon her and for all her adult problems. She almost detested her inner child.

I began an intense process to have Sally slowly recover from this injury. Before I gave Sally her next assignment, we prayed together. Let's do the same now:

> Dear God,
>
>   I am going inward on a journey of discovery. I beg for Your presence in this process. Give me the strength and foresight to learn and heal from this process. Help me to have the clear vision needed to get in touch with and embrace my inner child. I know You love my inner child, Lord, and I want to also.

My next step was letter-writing with a slightly different twist. Rather than having Sally just write out her feelings in letter form, which she had done several times, I asked her to write a letter to her inner child, doing the following:

a. Acknowledge her existence.
b. Give your inner child a name. (It could be a name you always wanted or a favorite nickname.)
b. Acknowledge that you abandoned her in your childhood (with the defense mechanisms we've discussed so far—denial and/or repression).
c. Explain (to the best of your ability) why you left her then. (For example, "Your pain was too much to bear so I bailed out. I'm sorry.")
d. Convince your inner child that you now want to be a friend and will try to unconditionally love her.
e. Close the letter, pledging your support for her, promising to include her in your everyday life.

Sally's letter might help you write your own if you're having problems thinking of things to say.

Dear Little Sally,

I know you exist now. I know that you're a hurt little girl and I'm sorry. I didn't mean to ignore you all these years. I was just afraid—afraid of you and all the pain you were in. I was afraid of what others would think if they saw you. Ken says the only way I am going to start feeling better is to take care of you. I believe him and I believe God. God loves you and so, I guess, do I. I will try to protect you and take care of you and love you. I'll do whatever I can to not leave you again. You will be welcome in my life. But I'm going to need some help. For that I'll rely on Jesus.

Your Friend,
Sally

Before you think this was a miraculous recovery, I'll tell you that it took several months and many sessions for Sally to get to this point. She had previously written lots of letters to her inner child pouring out her anger and frustration. In essence, she had to go through the exercises in the former chapters several times.

Now, write out your letter in the space provided on page 93.

If you find yourself having trouble writing this letter or feel that the exercise is merely an intellectual one, go back and reread the four previous chapters. This is especially helpful if you've experienced a severe childhood trauma. If writing this letter has evoked in you any overwhelming thoughts and feelings, call on that support list I constantly remind you about. And set aside this workbook for a day, at least, before proceeding to phase two.

Phase 2—Facing Your Inner Child

Take your above letter and go into a private room. Place two chairs facing each other. Find an object (a doll or stuffed animal works the best) and seat it

Dear _____,

_____

_____

_____

_____

_____

_____

_____

_____

_____

_____

_____

Sincerely,

_____

in one of the chairs. (And yes, men can do this. You are alone, after all.)

Next, sit yourself down in the facing chair and read your letter aloud to the object. Put as much feeling into your letter as you can. You have to convince your inner child that you are sincere.

Once you've done that, write your inner child another letter. This one should:

a. List all the messages you think your inner child has been hearing all these years. (For example, "You're bad. You caused all this pain. You're not a very good child. You're naughty. You're dirty.")

b. Next tell your inner child that all of these messages are false, lies straight from the father of lies.

c. Convince this inner child that he or she is good and welcome in your life today.
d. Tell the inner child that he or she is loved totally and unconditionally by God and by you. Remind your inner child that he or she is a part of God's beloved creation.
e. Pledge your undying love for this inner child and promise to protect and nurture him or her.
f. Close your letter with a promise that you will always return to your inner child. You won't abandon him or her now and you will be conscious of your inner child's existence every day of your life.

For an example of this second letter, let's see how Robert Benson wrote his. You'll recall that he was the workaholic who came to me for treatment of job burn-out—the result of childhood emotional neglect.

Dear Bobby,

I guess you've heard some pretty unfair things throughout your life. I've told you that you're no good, you can't do anything right, and that you are not as good as other people, so you have to try harder. Well, I've been wrong all these years. You aren't any worse than anyone else, I just thought you were. You're actually a very good little being, someone who is loved by God and by me. I'm telling you right now that I will try to protect you from the hurts and suffering in this world the best I can. I love you. I need you. I promise not to abandon you again.

Yours,
Robert

Now, write your second letter below.

✉

Dear _____,

_____

_____

_____

_____

_____

_____

_____

_____

_____

_____

Sincerely,

_____

Lay your letter and this workbook aside for another day. On the next day, return to the room you read your first letter in and place *three* chairs facing one another. Take the same object and put it in one of the chairs. Leave one chair vacant. Sit down in the third chair. Face the object and read your second letter aloud to it.

Again, put as much feeling as you can into your reading, be sincere and emotional. If you feel like crying, go ahead. If you feel like shouting, shout. (Warn the family beforehand, though, and ask them not to disturb you.) Let your feelings flow.

Next, pick up the object (remember, this is your inner child) and embrace it, holding it like you would a precious baby. Caress it like you would a small animal or an infant. This inner child has been bottled up and ignored inside you for a very long time, pour all your love and affection for it out in your actions now.

When you're ready, put the object down in the previously empty chair. Remove the first chair from your circle. This chair represents the dark, bound-up place where your inner child has been imprisoned. The new chair is where your inner child will be living from now on in your conscious mind! **Never again put the object down in that first chair.**

Children are very forgiving. Your inner child will forgive you for your abandonment. You must try, from now on, to hold true to your promise to love, cherish, and protect your inner child.

Permission to Feel

As a result of these exercises, you have given yourself permission to have feelings. Men may find this difficult because of society's conditioning, but with time, it will seem more natural.

If your inner child is to be healed and then stay healthy, you must allow yourself to feel. In the space below, write down what you are feeling at this point. Do not try to assess the validity of your feelings. All feelings are valid. If you're mad, say that. If you're sad, say so. If you're just emotional, put that down. If you're elated, write that out.

• •

I feel _____

_____

_____

• •

Now return to the *Feelings Log* discussed in chapter 3. Continue writing out your daily feelings. This should be much easier to do now, because you have acknowledged your emotions. Your expression of your feelings should flow more easily onto paper.

You will need the ability to acknowledge and label your feelings in Part II of this workbook. For this reason, it is essential that you keep your *Feelings Log* updated daily.

Also, from now on, please make the following proclamations aloud to yourself at the beginning or at the end of each day.

1. I am okay.
2. My inner child (my feelings) is an integral part of me, okay and necessary for my survival.
3. I love my inner child (I love my emotions).
4. I promise to protect my inner child from future injury by protecting and nurturing him or her.
5. I promise to combat any negative messages my inner child receives with positive messages, even in the face of adversity.

There are other players who will either help you or combat you as you try to live by the above proclamations, especially the fifth one. Once you know who they are, you can better accept or overcome their influence. Let's do that next.

Step Four

Meeting the Other Players

You take your seat in the darkened theater. A glance over the program reveals the woman lead, the hero, and the villain. The female lead is a favorite of yours, so is the hero—Dudley Doright. Uh-oh, Smedley is the villain, a wonderfully dastardly fellow. The curtain rises, Smedley has the girl tied on a train track. The organ plays, dum de dum, dum! Suddenly, Dudley rides in on his white horse.

A melodrama is entertaining simply because it is so exaggerated. And yet every day, every second of our lives, a mini-melodrama plays out in our minds. As an audience member, you recognize the villains and the heroes from the program. But as an individual, you don't know who the players are because you don't have a program. That's what I want to give you next. Our cast of players reads as follows:

Critical Parent
Good Parent
Rebellious Inner Child
Compliant Inner Child
Adult

And guess who the stars are. You, God through the Holy Spirit, and Satan. Before we go any further, take a guess at who plays what role. Write your answers below.

Critical Parent played by _____

Good Parent played by _____

Rebellious Inner Child played by _____

Compliant Inner Child played by _____

Adult played by _____

I will begin to assign the actors and actresses to these parts by reviewing each player's script and goals. Let's begin the analysis of our internal melodrama with prayer.

Dear God,

I know You are with me in my journey toward healing. I know You love my inner child. I will draw from this knowledge as I continue to love and appreciate this part of me. Now I need Your help and strength to help me see the influence Your Holy Spirit and Satan can have on my life. I need you to combat Satan's work within me. I know I cannot do that alone. I need You to help me see clearly—help me discern when it is Your Holy Spirit and when it is Satan talking to me. Thank You for being with me so far. Help me in this next step toward my recovery.

Critical Parent

If you haven't guessed already, the critical parent is the natural enemy of the inner child—the villain of your melodrama. Your villain's goal is the destruction of everything your inner child stands for: your emotional and spiritual health. Your critical parent will quash the creativity and spontaneity of your inner child.

Below is the beginning of a list of critical parent traits you can complete. Also are typical critical parent statements. Check those that sound familiar.

TRAITS OF A CRITICAL PARENT

Judgmental
Unforgiving
Cruel

_____

_____

_____

_____

_____

TYPICAL CRITICAL PARENT STATEMENTS

_____ You're not a good parent.

_____ You're not a good spouse.

_____ You're not good enough at your job.

_____ That other person is better than you.

_____ You're not a good person; you have bad thoughts and do bad things.

_____ Deep down, your feelings are not good. You can't show your true self to the world.

_____ Everybody else has it all together; you're the one who's a mess.

_____ You're not a good Christian.

The "You're not a good Christian" statement is a double-whammy. The critical parent voice loves to disguise itself as the voice of God. My patients frequently say they stop attending church or reading the Bible because of the intense negative feelings they get from critical parent messages. Or, if they don't stop attending church, they go and feel guilty the entire time.

Many people were raised under a judgmental upbringing. They grew up believing they were inferior and not loved by God. Now, they fear making mistakes, lest God severely punish them. They also believe God has abandoned them because they've been so bad.

Jennifer Laden was raised in a family where the children were "seen but not heard." She attended church every Sunday with her parents. One Sunday morning after church, she was playing in the chapel by herself.

A church elder came up to her and said, "You should be ashamed of yourself, Jennifer. You are disrespectful in the Lord's house. God is angry with those children who don't know their place."

Jennifer grew up with this sort of critical parent message repeated over and over: "God is angry with disrespectful people." She married and joined a church. At church, she threw herself into every activity she could, until she became overwhelmed with the demands of her family and church and suffered emotional collapse.

In therapy, Jennifer told me, "If I were a better Christian, I could do more. I could handle all the work the Lord wants me to do."

"But Jennifer, God doesn't want you to do everything. God wants you to be happy," I explained. "God gives you the knowledge to draw the line, to make limits on what you can physically and emotionally handle in your life. God gives you the strength to say no even to your church."

By now you may have surmised that Satan is at the root of the critical parent voice. He works through our critical parent voice—a composite of all the negative messages we have ever received—to try to undo everything God does through the Holy Spirit. Satan also works to try to undo our own well-being. In fact, if we continue to believe the critical parent messages, we will cease our spiritual journey. When we read the Scriptures, we will perceive judgment and condemnation. When we pray, we will believe God won't answer because we're not worthy of an answer. When we witness to others, we'll feel hypocritical. It's easy to see why Satan works through the critical parent voice, he wants to get you away from the Lord.

Discerning Your Own Critical Parent Voice

Before you begin to examine your critical parent voice, pray to God and ask for His assistance. Ask Him to reach into your unconscious mind and begin to expose this negative voice to you. Ask Him to empower you to deal with the critical parent.

Now complete the following sentence.

• •

I feel inferior because _____

_____

_____

_____

• •

Whatever you wrote in this sentence is a purely critical parent message. Just writing it out shows you've been listening to the critical parent voice inside you.

How do you tell if it's the critical parent speaking? Let's give it the test.

A. Is the sentence rational?
B. Is it something you can fix? (In other words, can you see *specific* ways to improve this inferiority?)

If you answer any of the above statements no, you can be sure it's a critical parent message.

"But," you might protest, "if I don't have any critical parent messages, what keeps me from messing up, getting into trouble? Isn't the critical parent just my conscience speaking to me?"

"Absolutely not!" I would answer.

Judgmental Versus Convictive Thought

The critical parent voice judges very harshly, allowing no room for mistakes. It expects perfection and then doesn't reward excellence. This voice accuses, saying, "You aren't good enough."

This is the first characteristic of a critical parent message, it's not rational. What exactly is a "good" Christian, daughter, friend, spouse, or parent? Where are the standards written in stone? Whose standards are they? What is good to one person may not be good to another.

The second characteristic of a critical parent message is that it is nebulous. It won't give you a definite way to rectify the situation. And since "good" or "bad" are internal labels, no outside behavior can change this. Thus, the more we try to be "good," the more we fail.

Convictive thought (thought through which God speaks to us), on the other hand, is very definitive and specific. It tells you exactly what you did wrong and then gives you a very definite way to rectify the error. If you commit adultery, you instantly know what you did wrong. There's no mistaking the offense. And, more so, you know what you need to do to rectify it: stop the adultery and ask for forgiveness.

So far you've only met one player in your melodrama—the villain. By the end of this chapter, you will have a complete program.

· ·

For this exercise, spend the next twenty-four hours listening to your critical parent voice. Carry a notebook with you. Every time you hear an internal critical or judgmental thought, jot it down. Again, these messages will usually sound like: "You're dumb. You can't do anything right. You're always messing up." And they will usually come following some event or behavior that didn't meet your expectations.

After this twenty-four hour period, review the messages in your log. How many times do the words *should, ought, always,* or *never* appear? _____ These words are a sure sign of a critical parent voice.

Examine the tone of the messages. Are they condemning, judging, or overly negative? ____ yes ____ no. If so, again, this is the critical parent voice.

How do you feel after reading these messages? _____
_____
_____

Your feelings are exactly those you unconsciously felt when your inner child heard the negative messages the first time. And they are the feelings you continue to have because you've internalized the messages and Satan has kept them alive.

Now, treat these messages as if they've been stated to you by another person. What kind of a person would say these things? Write a paragraph describing this type of a person below. Use lots of adjectives and descriptions.

_____

_____

_____

_____

_____

_____

Now write a paragraph, describing Satan as you have come to understand and know him through your spiritual teaching.

_____

_____

_____

_____

_____

See any similarity? _____ yes _____ no   There should be some. This is the voice you have been allowing to direct your life to a large degree!

• •

How do you like being directed by a liar? Satan is the force behind the critical parent voice, and Satan is a liar. Each critical parent statement you wrote in your notebook was a lie.

Some readers may now be hearing the message, "If you get rid of your critical parent voice, you will be directionless. Your behavior will be out of control." Do not listen to this lie. You will not be directionless; the next player will be there to guide you.

For this next exercise, we will symbolically get rid of the critical parent voice. Begin with another prayer. Ask God to stand by your side and to empower you to be strong and convicted to carry out this exercise.

• •

1. On a separate sheet of paper, draw a picture of your critical parent. Draw whatever image comes to mind. It can be a face or a symbol. If you can't think of anything to draw, simply write "Critical Parent" on the paper.

2. On another sheet of paper write "God" in big letters. You can even draw a picture, if you want to, of what God means to you.

3. Now tape both sheets of paper side by side on a wall.

4. Stand up, facing the papers. Make sure you remain standing throughout this entire exercise. (Note: if you can't stand because of physical illness, prop yourself up against a chair, or raise yourself on a chair higher than you normally sit.)

5. Look intently at the sheet of paper with "God" on it. Draw strength and love from God. Think about Him empowering you. Think about His undying, unconditional love for you. His love for you will never depend upon your performance or mistakes.

6. When ready, shift your eyes to the Critical Parent paper, begin to speak to it:

a. "I know you've been operating in my life and I know what you've been trying to do, to slowly destroy me and my inner child and my relationship with God."

b. "I am taking back the power I gave you to run my life. I no longer will believe your lies or deceptions!"

c. "I cast you away in the name of Jesus!"

If you have any doubts as you say these things to your symbolic critical parent, just look back at the God paper for strength and continue.

7. Take this Critical Parent paper off the wall. Tear it into small, tiny pieces and throw it away.

8. Return to the God paper. Keep this paper up in this room as you progress through this workbook. You can look at it when you need strength. (Remember, though, that the paper only *symbolizes* God. You still need to pray for His support.)

9. Say a prayer to God and thank Him for His help.

• •

Throughout the rest of your life, this critical parent voice will try to raise its ugly head over and over. Each time it does, ask for God's help, and remember that you threw this critical parent away.

Good Parent Voice

The good parent, on the other hand, is the friend and parent of your inner child. It is the voice of God through the Holy Spirit. Jesus promised this help to His disciples, "But the Helper, the Holy Spirit, whom the Father will send in My name, He will teach you all things, and bring to your remembrance all things that I said to you" (John 14:26).

This is the voice that we want to accompany us throughout our lives and in our relationships with others.

What are the characteristics of the good parent? Think back to any adult who had a positive influence in your life. List all the characteristics this person had.

• •

CHARACTERISTICS OF A GOOD PARENT

Dependable
Comforting
Supportive
Kind

_____

_____

_____

_____

_____

• •

I hope you named at least the following three characteristics in some fashion:

nurturer
protector
instructor

If you were unable to list these characteristics, or if you didn't have such a role model, this section may be more difficult. But you will still learn how to discern and listen to your good parent voice by the end of this workbook.

Let's take each of these three main traits of the good parent and describe them, both in terms of your childhood experience and in terms of what God provides.

Nurturer

First and foremost, parents must nurture their young. They must take care of all the physical and emotional needs of the children. Remember the needs I listed in chapter 6? The basic physical needs are food, water, clothes, shelter, and medical care. The emotional needs include acceptance, love, and significance. If one or more of these needs is not met, the child suffers neglect.

• •

Were these needs met in your childhood? _____ yes _____ no

List those needs which were met.

_____

_____

_____

_____

_____

_____

_____

_____

_____

List those needs which were not met.

_____

_____

_____

• •

Whatever exists in your second list is probably what you have been try-ing to fulfill through external behaviors or activities, such as workaholism, codependent relationships, drugs, alcoholism, or material acquisitions. If you haven't anything in that second list, take a hard look. You may be experiencing denial, for there are no perfect parents on earth. God is the only perfect par-ent. The rest of us are human beings and as such, we make mistakes.

Now picture God as the ultimate nurturer. Begin this exercise by asking God to reveal His nurturing side to you.

• •

List the ways that God nurtured others. (Think of biblical ac-counts as well as contemporary examples, such as God feeding and protecting the Hebrews as they wandered through the wilderness.)

_____

_____

_____

_____

List the ways God has been a nurturer to you. (For example, God comforts me through prayer as well as through other people.)

_____

_____

_____

_____

_____

Look back at the list of unmet needs. Pick out the emotional ones and list those that God can fulfill for you. (For example, God can take care of my self-validation needs.)

_____

_____

_____

• •

God created your inner child. God loves and desires to nurture your inner child. However, He can only nurture you if you foster an intimate relationship with Him, which I will talk about more in chapter 10.

Protector

The good parent also has the job of keeping the child safe and free from danger. The protecting good parent interprets the environment around the child and protects the child from emotional harm.

• •

Think back to your childhood. List the physical dangers you were exposed to as a child.

_____

_____

_____

_____

_____

Were you protected from these physical dangers as a child?
____ yes ____ no ____ sometimes   Which ones were you not protected from and what were the circumstances, as you remember them?

_____

_____

_____

List the emotional dangers you were exposed to as a child.

_____

_____

_____

_____

Were you protected from these emotional dangers as a child?
____ yes ____ no ____ sometimes   Which ones were you not protected from and what were the circumstances, as you remember them? _____

_____

_____

• •

Now ask God to reveal His protector side to you and fill in the following exercises.

• •

List the ways God protects others. (For example, God protected Hezekiah from the king of Assyria in 2 Kings 18–19.)

_____

_____

_____

_____

List the ways God has been a protector to you. (For example, when I was afraid to undergo anesthesia at the dentist's office, I prayed and God gave me the inner strength to endure the operation, and without fear.)

_____

_____

_____

_____

_____

List those emotional dangers that God can protect you from, especially the ones you were not shielded from in childhood.

_____

_____

_____

_____

• •

Many abuse or neglect victims protest this last exercise. "Where was God when I was being hurt as a child!" they cry. Again, we as mortal beings, cannot answer that. We can't even conceive His actions because we see such a small portion of His overall plan for the universe. However, I firmly believe He protects the inside of the child while the outside is in danger by giving us natural defense mechanisms like denial and repression.

This is also why you are able to work in this workbook. God has preserved and protected your inner child and will continue to do so.

Instructor

All children must learn right from wrong. The parents are responsible to teach this. As I mentioned before, there are three ways we learn: by the spoken word, behaviors, and modeling. Modeling is the most effective way to teach a child, with behavior next in importance, followed by the spoken word.

For this reason, we must form an idea of what a good parent instructor is using the modeling we've witnessed in our lives.

Think back to a parent or another adult in your childhood whom you think modeled the way a good parent should instruct. Now list at least five personality traits of this person (for example: understanding, firm, loving).

• •

1. _____

2. _____

3. _____

4. _____

5. _____

How did this person provide loving and guiding instruction? Describe the incident you remember and how he or she helped you learn. _____

_____

_____

_____

• •

If you could not recall a good parent model in your childhood, fear not. God is the ultimate example of what a good parent should be. He is the best model by which we can form a concept of how our good parent voice should sound.

• •

List the ways God has been an instructor to others in biblical or modern times. (Perhaps the most famous example is in Exodus 20 where God gave the Ten Commandments to Moses for the people of Israel.)

_____

_____

_____

_____

_____

List the ways God has been an instructor for you. (For example, I often pray to God before and during sessions for instruction on where to go with my patients. Any insight I have, I attribute to God.)

_____

_____

_____

_____

_____

• •

God is actually an instructor to your inner child and He speaks to it through the Holy Spirit—the good parent voice within you. Your inner child deserves and needs this instruction. As we proceed in this workbook, you will learn how to listen to this voice at the exclusion of the detrimental critical parent voice.

The following are examples of critical parent and good parent messages that your inner child might hear. See how well you can discriminate between them. If you believe it's your critical parent voice speaking, write CP beside the statement. If you believe it is your good parent voice, write GP beside the statement.

• •

1. _____ You're not a good enough Christian.
2. _____ It might help you to feel closer to God if you prayed to Him more.
3. _____ You really loused up that test; you're a failure.
4. _____ Yes, you fell short this time. You do make mistakes and you may be weak in some areas, but inside you're still a worth-

while person. Next time you can study harder and maybe
do better.

5. ____ You are not as good as she is.

6. ____ She may look and dress better than you, but that doesn't
mean she's any better inside than you are. You are both
equal in God's eyes.

7. ____ You really botched up this job. How could you be so stupid?

8. ____ Yes, you made a mistake. But everyone makes mistakes. You
can try to minimize them, but you are still worthy in God's
eyes.

9. ____ You just yelled at your wife. You are a lousy husband.

10. ____ You've just yelled at your wife. You know what you did
wrong. You need to go back and apologize to her for yelling and then talk over your disagreement. Doing so doesn't
mean you were wrong to feel the way you did.

• •

Can you see a pattern to your CP statements? The critical parent voice is
not very imaginative. In fact it sounds like a broken record. (Did you notice
this in the log you kept on critical parent messages?)

Before we go on and meet the other players in our melodrama, let's pray
that God will let His Holy Spirit work daily in our lives through our good
parent voice. You can use the following prayer or think one up of your own.

Our heavenly Father,

You created us in Your image. You breathed life into us
through Your Holy Spirit. You loved us before we were conceived
and born. Lord, our past sometimes confuses us. People let us
down. Parents knowingly or unknowingly hurt us and this leaves us
confused and frightened on the inside. But I know You never
stopped loving me. Even when I couldn't hear Your voice because

of confused childhood messages, You were there. Lord, I pray now that I may again learn to hear Your nurturing, protecting, and instructing voice. I need You, as my good parent, to complete my recovery. I pray that You will hold me when I'm frightened, that You will protect me when I'm in danger, and that You will instruct me when I'm confused. Lord, I know at times I may not feel Your love and presence, especially when I'm depressed or upset. But let me believe, if only intellectually, that You are always there as my good parent voice until my emotions are stabilized. Then let me feel Your presence. Thank you, Lord.

Rebellious Inner Child

Like a physical child, the inner child has two parts—a rebellious inner child and a compliant inner child. The rebellious inner child wants to do everything contrary to what he or she is told to do by the parenting voices. Even though irritating at times, this player plays a very crucial role. It is only through the rebellious inner child that we are able to foster change in our lives. And change allows us to grow and learn.

In some people, this rebellious inner child will dominate. These people will always protest, always want to rebel against whatever they are told to do. They don't feel they want or need love and acceptance.

Remember Phil Sanderling? He constantly ran from relationships with women when they got serious. In this case his compliant and rebellious inner children were at odds.

His compliant inner child wanted love and acceptance. So he pursued relationships with women. But when he got that acceptance, his rebellious inner child said, "No, I don't need anyone. This is too confining. I've got to leave now." And he would.

• •

See if you can think of some ways your rebellious inner child has presented itself to you recently in a relationship. Write them down.

(For example, "My husband came home today expecting dinner on the table. It wasn't and, by my attitude, I dared him to make a comment.")

_____

_____

_____

_____

_____

Perhaps your situation might not have to do with a relationship, but what about work or your daily routine? What have you wanted to rebel against recently? (For example, "Yesterday morning I didn't want to get out of bed. Part of me wanted to sleep in and miss work.") __

_____

_____

• •

The Compliant Inner Child

The compliant inner child is the opposite of the rebellious inner child. He or she craves love and fears abandonment. The compliant inner child wants to please others so that he or she will receive that acceptance and validation.

Think how your compliant inner child has shown itself in your behaviors and thoughts recently. Robert Benson wrote out the following paragraph.

"I find myself working long hours and doing a task over and over to please my boss and make myself look good to my coworkers. I guess this is my compliant inner child wanting validation and acceptance from them."

Now it's your turn.

_____

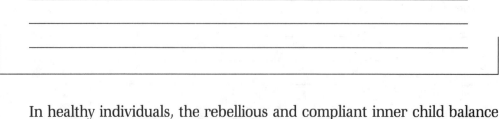

In healthy individuals, the rebellious and compliant inner child balance one another. They alternate dominancy, depending upon the incident and keep each other in check. We experience problems with these two aspects of ourselves when one excludes or suppresses the other.

This frequently happens with a wounded inner child. In abuse or neglect victims, the rebellious inner child can become stronger as it protects the weaker, compliant inner child.

"If no one shows me love, then I don't need anyone's love" is the message this inner child operates on. In particularly severe cases, this rebellious inner child can be so dominant, a persona can almost act cruel and non-feeling. He or she can't even conceive sympathy or empathy for others.

Unfortunately, this type of individual can become the hardened ruthless criminal. It's a sad story that's played out over and over in our courts. It can generally be traced back to a wounded inner child during childhood.

The Adult

The last player in our melodrama is the adult. This part of ourselves performs primarily in our outer self and acts as a mediator between the inner child and parenting voices. The adult's job is to shield the inner child from the outside world and to relay messages to and from the inner child.

The Curtain Rises, the Melodrama Begins

To see how all these players might interact in a normal everyday situation, let's look at the following incident.

You are at a grocery store and about to pay for all your items at the cashier, but you're having trouble coming up with the exact change.

The cashier says, "Can't you speed it up? Others are waiting in line. You're really causing a lot of trouble here."

Your compliant inner child is instantly hurt. Someone doesn't like you or your actions.

Your rebellious inner child wants to drop to the floor, kicking and screaming, or lash back with something like, "Who cares if I don't give you the exact change instantly? I can take as long as I want."

Your critical parent voice says, "Boy, you're a dunce. You can't do anything right. You're really messing up this time. Everyone is staring."

Your good parent voice says, "Yes, you might be taking too long to find the right change, but you're still okay. Just because this lady is acting this way toward you doesn't mean you are any less of a person."

And finally, your adult voice intervenes, "Look, I know you are hurt inside, but I don't want you to react emotionally right now. It's okay to hurt inside, but let me take over and handle this situation and get us out of this line."

Then you will calmly hand over the correct change and take your purchases. You might respond to the cashier by apologizing for taking so long, or just ignore the situation and go your merry way.

This is how the melodrama *should* play out. Unfortunately, the ideal doesn't often happen. Generally, we operate from the premise of only one player.

Now think back to a recent incident when you had a difficult interaction with someone. See if you can dissect the voices that were at work within you and write out the script below.

• •

Incident (a brief synopsis of what happened): _____

_____

_____

_____

_____

_____

Compliant Inner Child: _____

_____

_____

Rebellious Inner Child: _____

_____

_____

Critical Parent: _____

_____

_____

Good Parent: _____

_____

_____

Adult: _____

_____

_____

Which voice dominated the others?

_____

• •

Often one particular voice invokes the opposite voice in another. This characterizes a lot of relationship communication.

For example, if we present a critical parent voice to another person, we will probably invoke that person's rebellious inner child voice. Unfortunately, this is the most common type of communication in the world today: critical parent to rebellious inner child. You can readily see how futile this communication pattern can become.

In the above scenario, the cashier communicated from her critical parent. If you are like most people in this world, you, too, would have responded from the rebellious inner child by lashing back. This is because the rebellious inner child will always try to protect the compliant inner child.

Can you now begin to see how powerful this Inner Child therapy can be for relationships? I hope so.

I first noticed the players at work inside me through my relationship with my wife, Mary Jo. One evening I came home very late from a seminar. Mary Jo did not have dinner waiting for me.

"How come dinner's not ready?" I asked. Now this statement could be innocent enough, asking just a simple question, except that I acted like I expected it to be ready. I was sending the critical parent message, "You should have had my dinner ready."

Mary Jo picked up on this critical tone and answered from her rebellious child voice, "If you knew the day I had, you wouldn't be so inconsiderate. I couldn't know when to fix your dinner."

It's easy to see how this interchange could have escalated, especially if my critical parent voice kept invoking Mary Jo's rebellious child response. Such situations can even reverse. Mary Jo could have started saying critical parent messages to me, which would have ignited my rebellious inner child voice.

The key to improving communication within relationships is to know our players, recognize the players speaking in the other person, and then appropriately manage these players.

9

Step Five
Forgiving

The very last phase in Inner Child work is forgiveness. After the client has embraced his or her own inner child, I have him or her totally and unconditionally forgive everyone involved in wounding the inner child—including ourselves.

Forgiving is one of the hardest things to do, but if the patient doesn't take this step, the therapy will never be finished. The pain will not be resolved, and the resultant bitterness will control the patient and his or her inner child.

A Background in Forgiveness

Think back to your childhood. What do you remember about forgiveness in your family? Was spiritual or practical forgiveness modeled? To help you remember, check the statements that apply to your situation.

• •

1. ____ My father had no problems asking for forgiveness when he had wronged someone.
2. ____ My mother had no problems asking for forgiveness when she had wronged someone.
3. ____ The children were encouraged to ask for and receive forgiveness when they did something wrong.

4. _____ Grown-ups never asked for forgiveness because they never did anything wrong.

5. _____ Forgiveness was never mentioned or discussed in my family.

6. _____ Once something was done and forgiven, we were required to forget about it and never mention it again.

7. _____ I heard this phrase or something like it at least once in my family: "I can never forgive _____ for _____. What he or she did was unforgivable."

8. _____ We were very open in my family. We talked about issues that needed forgiveness and tried to resolve them as a family unit.

9. _____ There were things I did in childhood for which I don't feel forgiven.

10. _____ My family held grudges.

11. _____ We were taught there are wrongs for which people can't be forgiven.

• •

Now describe what you remember about the concept of forgiveness in your family. Either do it generally or pick a specific incident that you recall. Describe how forgiveness was handled. (For example, I remember breaking a lamp when I was a child. I was punished and my parents were mad at me for a long time. I guess you could say forgiveness didn't come easy in my house.)

• •

_____

_____

_____

_____

_____

_____

_____

Based on this observation, would you say you received a good modeling of forgiving behavior? ____ yes ____ no.

• •

- Do you understand what forgiveness is? ____ yes ____ no
- Do you practice it on a daily basis? ____ yes ____ no
- If you answered affirmatively to the above questions, the exercises in this chapter should not prove too difficult. However, if you answered no to any of the questions, you, like most of us, may not have received a good example of forgiving behavior. You will need a review of some of the basics.

False Forgiveness Versus True Forgiveness

False forgiveness is trying to forgive before coming to terms with the act requiring forgiveness.

I recall a wife who came to me for counseling with her husband, whom she had discovered in an affair.

"I've forgiven Harry for that," she said. This was our first session, so I asked her when she had found out about Harry's affair.

"Oh, last week," she answered.

Right then I suspected she was operating under false forgiveness.

I have a person forgive only when he or she has completely worked through the pain, sorrow, and suffering associated with the offense. But before we even attempt this forgiveness, I give them a little background in what forgiveness really means.

The Points of Forgiveness

1. First and foremost, forgiveness is for the benefit of the forgiver, not the forgiven. The price we pay for not forgiving is anger, which can easily turn into resentment and bitterness. Unresolved anger has been associated with a variety of physical ailments including heart problems, cancer, hormone instabilities, stress induced illnesses, and a reduced immunity to other diseases.

Forgiveness cleanses us and brings closure to painful events. Also, psychologically, forgiveness disempowers the perpetrator. By choosing to forgive those who wrong us, we end their influence over us.

2. We are spiritually empowered by God to forgive. When Peter asked Jesus how much one should forgive, Jesus' answer was seventy times seven, meaning not 490 times, but that a person should forgive endlessly. During His final moments of suffering on the cross, Jesus asked His Father to forgive the perpetrators.

Christ Jesus' example is to practice forgiveness every second of our lives. In fact, it is only by forgiving others that we are forgiven: "For if you forgive men their trespasses, your heavenly Father will also forgive you. But if you do not forgive men their trespasses, neither will your Father forgive your trespasses" (Matt. 6:14–15).

3. Choosing to forgive the perpetrator does not mean you have to reestablish a relationship with him or her. You can choose never to see that person again and still have resolved the trauma he or she caused you. You don't have to face this person in order to forgive.

4. Choosing to forgive is an act of our will, not of our feelings. We may forgive in spite of our feelings, to continue our recovery. After we have forgiven, we may still experience anger when thinking about the wrong. This is common. We can ask God's help, then, in dealing with the anger. But our anger does not mean we haven't forgiven.

5. You only have to forgive the perpetrator once. You don't have to go back and forgive each time you remember the trauma or hurts you suffered. Think of forgiveness like baptism. Once you've been baptized, you need not do it again. Once you've forgiven a perpetrator for a specific event or incident, you're done with it. You may have to forgive this perpetrator for other acts that have caused you pain, but you only forgive an act once.

6. Forgiving does not validate the act as right. Nor does it accept responsibility for the act. If a wife yells at her husband, he may feel convicted or empowered to forgive her for yelling, but he is not saying that her yelling was appropriate.

To put it another way, forgiving does not validate a crime, nor release the criminal from the responsibility for paying for that crime through judicial sentencing. It simply forgives the criminal for committing the crime.

7. Forgiving does not mean that you are becoming powerless. We forgive out of a position of spiritual power. We human beings tend to think that if we forgive we are showing our weakness—allowing the other person to get away with the crime. Not so. Forgiveness is a separate action that is primarily for your benefit.

8. Forgiveness does not depend on the other person's response. In fact, you may not get a positive reaction from the forgiven individual if you choose to forgive in person, particularly if that person does not feel he or she has done anything wrong.

Why Forgive?

"Why do I have to forgive my uncle?" Sally Dansen asked. "He molested me!"

"I know and you have every right to be angry," I answered. "But, Sally, believe me, if you decide not to forgive him, that act will never be resolved in your mind. It will continue to plague and control you. You will never be free from him until you forgive. Is that what you want?"

"No," she answered, tears welling up in her eyes. "But I'm still afraid of him, I don't even want to see him again."

"I'm not asking you to contact your uncle, you can forgive him, symbolically, in my office."

"I'm still afraid."

"I know and for that reason I will be here with you. I will protect you. Do you know who else will be here?"

"Who?"

"God, of course. He will be here and will give you the strength to carry out this forgiveness."

"Okay, so what do I do?"

"Well, first we have to know exactly what it is you are forgiving."

Tasks Toward Forgiveness

Task 1: List and acknowledge the traumas and hurts you need to forgive.

In the space provided below, list all the hurts and traumas you have thought of up to this point in the workbook. Sally's specific traumas were the repeated sexual abuse by her uncle and her parents' neglect of her during that time.

What specific childhood memories came up as a result of reading chapters 4, 5, and 6, on the specific hurts our inner child experiences? List them below.

_____

_____

_____

_____

_____

_____

_____

_____

Task 2: List the perpetrators for those hurts and traumas. Of course, Sally had listed her uncle, her mother, and her father in this second list. For each hurt you listed above, name the person who caused those hurts.

_____

_____

_____

_____

_____

Task 3: Acknowledge your feelings. Look back at the above two lists. Allow yourself to feel anger, remorse, sadness, rage, pain. Write your feelings in a paragraph below.

Sally's paragraph read as follows:

> I feel really angry, really mad at my uncle. How could he do this to me? I was just a defenseless little girl. How could he ruin my life this way? It isn't fair; it just isn't fair! I'm really upset with my parents. Why didn't they see what was happening? Why didn't they protect me? And I'm really angry with God. How could He abandon me? How could He let this happen?

Now it's your turn.

I feel _____

_____

_____

_____

_____

The last few sentences of Sally's paragraph are clues to someone else you must put on your list to forgive—God.

"God?" Sally asked. "How can I forgive God? He does no wrong."

"True," I answered. "But you are mad at Him. You stated it in your paragraph. Until you resolve this anger, you will feel resentful and bitter toward God. These feelings will block your relationship with Him."

"But forgive God? It sounds so, so disrespectful."

"It doesn't have to make sense, Sally. We often get mad at God. Why did that person have to die? Why does the world have so much pain and suffering? The list is endless. But, you see, forgiveness is for *your* benefit, not God's. He wants you to forgive Him, for your sake," I said.

Likewise, if you find yourself mad at God, add Him to your list. Your forgiveness of Him is infinitely critical if you have any desire for a close relationship with Him. Forgiving God isn't saying He was wrong or that He really did abandon you. It is getting rid of your anger toward Him once you've acknowledged it.

Task 4: Forgive.

There are two major approaches to this. One involves making contact with the person you need to forgive. The other involves role-playing the encounter. There are very specific guidelines for each approach.

1. Approach One

I suggest this approach only for relationships you want to improve, not for victims to use with perpetrators of childhood or adulthood trauma. If you elect to contact the person you wish to forgive, I recommend you do so in writing, especially if the hurt was a big one. First write a letter to that person, pouring out all your feelings, especially your anger. Then destroy the letter. Give yourself some breathing space. Then write another letter. Make sure you have acknowledged, very specifically, the hurt you are forgiving. Close your letter with a pledge that you want the relationship to continue and that you care deeply for this person. It may help to have someone from your support list edit your letter so you say what you need to with the right attitude, not, "I forgive you for being such a moron!"

When you feel the letter is ready, send it to the person you are forgiving. Once you've mailed it, let it go. In other words, do not expect an answer, especially a remorseful one—your forgiven may not feel he or she has done anything wrong. So don't be crushed if the person comes back saying he or she doesn't need this forgiveness. Remember, you can't expect him or her to understand your need to forgive—the forgiveness is for your benefit.

2. Approach Two

The second approach is the one I recommend for those with a recovering wounded inner child. It may be the best way to deal with hurts from your parents. It's definitely the approach to take when you've suffered physical or sexual abuse. This is the tack I took with Sally and her uncle.

In these situations, I have my patients role-play the forgiveness. First I ask my patients to go home and write out a complete letter, detailing the trauma and feelings. I tell them to state in the letter that they are giving the responsibility for this act back to the perpetrator.

Sally's first letter looked like the following.

✉

Dear Uncle John,

You have victimized me. You have taken advantage of a defenseless little girl. All these years I have taken the blame for what you did. I even abandoned the little girl inside me because of what you did. It was you who caused this. I've let you and the effects of what you did to me run my life up to this point.

I hereby denounce what you've done. I carry no responsibility for what happened. I give you back responsibility for your actions against me. And from here on, I am responsible for my own life.

Sally

Write your own letter to each person on your list in Task 2. Use the space below to write the letter to the most serious perpetrator.

✉

Dear _____,

_____

_____

_____

_____

_____

_____

_____

_____

_____

_____

                                    _____

For the next phase, preface this exercise with a prayer to God for strength and conviction. Ask Him to help you face this perpetrator and help you forgive him or her completely. (Yes, even if it's God Himself you are forgiving, ask Him for help. He will!)

Now find a comfortable place to sit. Close your eyes and picture the most serene place you know of. It could be a forest, a beach, or a mountain meadow. Ellen, my client who went through this Inner Child therapy at the age of seventy, pictured a country road.

This place you have in your mind is your secret place. I will have you refer back to this place several times throughout the rest of the workbook. Ellen described her country road as follows.

The country road I am walking down is narrow and seldom-used. I remember it from somewhere, far back in my childhood. The road is red clay and sand. It is lined with wildflowers and grass waving in the breeze. Cottonwoods hang over the sides of the road, filtering the sunlight through their branches. Butterflies flit among the flowers and birds chirp from the trees. This is the one place from my childhood that invokes feelings of peace and tranquility.

Describe your special place in detail below.

My serene place looks like _____

_____

_____

_____

_____

_____

_____

_____

If it is a real place from a childhood memory, that's fine. If it's a made-up place, that's also okay. Certain rules apply to this special place.

Rule 1: This is your place and only your place. No one can come here except by your invitation and escort. In fact, I will have you pretend you are bringing certain people to this place, blindfolded, so they cannot return without your help.

Rule 2: This is your turf. Whenever you bring someone here you are the one in power. You have control over the situation.

Rule 3: When your world gets particularly stressful or harried, you can close your eyes and go to this place for refreshment and tranquility.

Rule 4: It is a given that God knows about this place and can accompany you, at your invitation.

Rule 5: It is not a given that Satan knows about this place. He is *never* invited to accompany you here.

Picture yourself taking God and whomever you are forgiving to this special place. You find a nice place to sit down and remove the blindfold from the person you are forgiving—the perpetrator. God is sitting on your right, the perpetrator on your left. Both are facing you.

Look at God first, draw strength from Him as you do. Now look at the perpetrator. If you start to feel afraid, look back at God. He will be there to protect you.

Look the perpetrator directly in the eyes and then begin to read your letter out loud to him or her. Put as much feeling as you can in the letter. If you waiver or feel frightened, switch over to God and ask for His help.

Once you've done this, you have freed yourself from the guilt you've been carrying around all these years. Now you are able to forgive this person, with God's help.

Ask God to help you forgive. Then look at the perpetrator and say: "I know what you did wasn't right. I don't agree with it. But, because you are one of God's creations (even if you are not a Christian), I completely and totally forgive you for what you did to me."

Once you've done this, picture yourself getting up, blindfolding the perpetrator, and walking him or her away from this special place forever. You will never bring the perpetrator back to this special place, unless you think of another act for which you need to forgive him or her. As you walk away, remember to thank God for supporting and empowering you.

In the forgiveness process, there is one final step I have my patients do. I ask them to bury the letter they read to the perpetrator. This serves to close the issue once and for all. I did this with Robert Benson and we had an actual funeral outside my office. If you choose to do this you will be symbolically burying the trauma. Then, every time it rears its ugly head again, you can say, "I buried that issue. It's over and done with."

To do this, tear out the letter you wrote above. Fold it up and bury it outside.

If you have performed these exercises and experienced feelings of fear, call your closest support person. Arrange for a time he or she can be present at your home. Then restage the entire exercise, with him or her participating. If you're frightened again, hold his or her hand for support. If you're still afraid or distraught, call a professional counselor for help with this exercise.

I was present when Sally read her letter to her absent uncle. She was terrified when I told her she was taking her uncle by the hand, blindfolded, to her secret place. It took several attempts for Sally to understand that her uncle couldn't hurt her now—that she was about to cast him from her life for good.

Approach Two over Approach One for Inner Child Trauma

The reason I don't recommend trying to make contact with the actual perpetrator for inner child traumas is that the perpetrator will usually deny the incident or incidents. If the situation was buried deeply in the patient, beneath a layer of denial, this reaction could throw the patient back under that denial layer.

This is what happened with Sheila Cronkhite. You'll recall that Sheila had an abusive husband. Through therapy she also discovered that her mother had repeatedly physically abused her. Eventually, Sheila came to terms with that trauma. She left her husband and moved to another state, away from my clinic. A friend recommended that Sheila make contact with her mother and resolve the matter.

When Sheila did so, her mother denied anything like that had ever happened. Sheila was devastated. All her pain and suffering were for naught. Her denial layer came back up.

She called me later, "I'm so relieved to finally know that all that stuff never happened. I was just so confused and distraught, I guess I made it all up."

Sheila had abandoned her inner child again! I don't know if she ever recognized this.

So, don't take the risk and face the perpetrator with your letter of forgiveness—especially if it is a parent. Two points that need to be considered here are:

1. If you are under the care of a professional psychotherapist, make sure they know you are working through this workbook.

But follow their advice on this matter. They can help you determine whether or not you should confront your perpetrator.

2. Obviously, a perpetrator's asking for forgiveness is different. But I still recommend the victim consult a counselor to be clear on all of the complex issues.

Forgiving the perpetrator will be more effective if you do it symbolically. There will be a noticeable difference in you—you won't be as intimidated as before. The perpetrator will no longer have any control over you.

If you don't forgive, you may continue to be influenced by the inner child trauma. And you will likely continue to be plagued by this perpetrator's influence over your life.

Before I close this first part of the workbook, I want to reinforce that I am not searching for problems in your past. If you absolutely couldn't come up with any hurts or traumas that needed forgiving in this chapter, fear not. I am not on a "wild goose chase," looking for something that simply isn't there. Be aware, though, of the power of denial and repression. Even a subtle injury like no self-validation from your father is an act that needs forgiving and resolving so it won't fester and hurt you as an adult.

That's what the second part of this workbook is about—you and your relationships today, how you can put all this together to work for a better you and better relationships.

MAINTAINING RECOVERY

——

Living with Your Players and Improving Relationships

Step Six

Improving Your Relationship with God

10

Relationships are the only means of emotional survival we have on this planet. They are the vehicle through which we love and learn, and through which we pass on our love and learnings.

Before I get into the specific, practical ways you can use what you learned in Part One about your inner child and your other players, I want you to do a priority exercise.

Look at the following list of persons with whom you have relationships today. Put this list in priority order. Rate the relationship you consider most important "1" and the least important "9."

• •

PRIORITY OF MY RELATIONSHIPS

_____ Coworkers	_____ Wife or Husband	_____ Brother or Sister
_____ Parent(s)	_____ Boss	_____ God
_____ Children	_____ Friend(s)	_____ Myself

• •

Obviously, each person will have a different set of priorities for his or her relationships. However, the closer you move toward putting God first, yourself second, and your spouse (if you have one) third, the better your life will be.

This is exactly the order that God instructs us to take, but it is the hardest to maintain. In a family, who typically gets the most energy and attention? The children. The relationship between husband and wife should come before the parents' relationships with the children because children learn by example. If they are not shown a happy marriage, children will not know what constitutes a happy union in their adult life.

They also need to see us take care of ourselves and our relationship with God. However, "self" usually gets the last priority. We tend to sacrifice ourselves at a very high price. Our needs go unmet while we struggle to meet the needs of others around us.

To overcome this we need to first shore up ourselves. If we are healthy, our other relationships will naturally improve. Other people will be less able to affect our emotional state when we heal our inner child.

Most of us gauge our feelings by our interactions with other people. If a person sends us negative, critical messages, our feelings about ourselves can become negative and critical. Conversely, if we're around someone who is nurturing and encouraging, our feelings and confidence soar. Thus, our emotions fluctuate based on how others relate to us. We've shown this phenomenon in the following diagram.

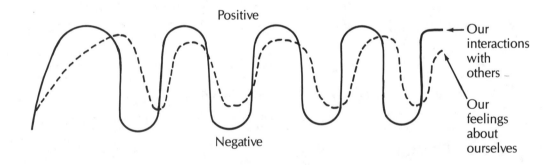

How Interactions Affect Our Negative Feelings

Inner child thinking helps to straighten out our emotional feelings. We are not as affected by others' perceptions because we can combat their critical messages with our own good parent messages from the Holy Spirit. In the best of circumstances, we will feel the same about ourselves no matter whom we come up against in the world. And our diagram would look like this one.

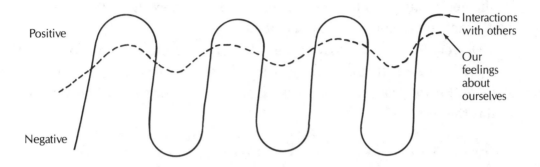

Positive

Interactions with others

Our feelings about ourselves

Negative

Our Interactions and Feelings with a Healed Inner Child

In the next few chapters, I hope to give you very practical ways you can achieve this "even keel" approach to your relationships, using the players inside you. And one of the most effective ways to achieve this is by a secure relationship with God.

· ·

OUR RELATIONSHIP WITH GOD

Did you put God as your number one priority on your list? _____ yes _____ no
Do you actually put Him number one above anyone else, including yourself? _____ yes _____ no

· ·

If you answered the above questions honestly, perhaps at least one of the answers was no. Very few of us really treat God as the most important person in our lives. We may go to church, read the Bible, and pray on a regular basis, but we frequently take our relationship with Him for granted.

In this chapter, I will show you how to use the players inside you to improve your relationship with God and how to maintain it in the top priority spot. But first, let's look at the history of your relationship with God.

History of This Relationship

The very first image we form of God is from our parents. As I mentioned in chapter 4, our parents are, to us, demigods. We perceive them as omnipotent, omnibenevolent, and omniscient.

Our parents model behavior we tend to associate with God's behavior. If they are loving, nurturing, and forgiving parents, then we grow to see God in that light. If they are critical, judgmental, and non-forgiving, then we think God is that way.

• •

To get a baseline on your perception of God, answer the following questions.

How do you see God? Describe Him in detail. (For example, do you see a loving, benevolent God with whom you have a personal relationship, or an imposing, intimidating being from whom you feel distant?) _____

_____

_____

_____

Now describe your father when you were growing up. _____

_____

_____

_____

Are there any similarities between your first two answers? ____ yes ____ no   If so, what are they? _____

_____

_____

_____

What are the main differences between your first two answers? ____

_____

_____

_____

Now describe your mother when you were growing up. _____

_____

_____

_____

Are there any similarities between your first and fifth answers?
_____ yes _____ no   If so, what are they? _____

_____

_____

_____

What are the main differences between your first and fifth answers?

_____

_____

_____

Describe how you think God feels about you. (For example, does He
love you no matter what you do or how you act? Or is He always
looking to catch you doing wrong in order to punish you?) _____

_____

_____

Describe how you think your father feels about you. (Does he approve
of you or is he disappointed?) _____

_____

_____

Describe how you think your mother feels about you. (Is she proud or
does she often seem disappointed in you?) _____

_____

_____

Did you notice any patterns to your answers to these final three questions? _____ yes _____ no   If so, what were they? (For example, your father feels you are not living up to his standards and he still corrects you on your mistakes. And you think God is also focusing on your mistakes.) _____

_____

_____

_____

_____

• •

Now give your answers to the "Sunday school test." Because many of us received most of our spiritual education in Sunday school, it's these facts that remain when we think and talk about God. However, for this workbook, I don't want Sunday school memorizations. Rather, I want your true feelings about God and your perception of Him.

What I mean by Sunday school answers are: "God is everywhere at all times. He sees me always. He is my protector and Savior." These answers are most certainly true, but they have come out in the vernacular of Sunday school and church teachings. I want your feelings about God in your own simple, easy-to-understand words. God loves us enough to want us to be honest in our answers and our feelings toward Him.

Go back again to questions one and eight. If your answers seem similar, even canned, bow your head in prayer and ask God to remove your Sunday-school glasses. Ask Him to reveal your unconscious thoughts to your conscious mind. Then ask and answer those questions again.

Don't be alarmed if your descriptions of God and your parents' descriptions were similar. That's natural, remember? However, if you formed a judgmental, critical view of God, based on your parents' example, I want you to change that view through the exercises in this chapter.

Our Present Day Relationship with God

What kind of relationship do you have with God? What messages are being relayed to your inner child? This may be difficult to perceive at first, but it is crucial for you to start discerning these messages. Consider what God said, what He looked like, and what your inner child heard. Write down what you think your unique inner child heard from your picture of God, following the example given.

God stood in front of me and said, "John, I'm disappointed in you. How could you be so unfeeling to Marge and the kids? You are not being a biblically correct father and husband these days."

God acted reproachful. He even shook His finger at me. He had a stern look on His face which frightened me.

The inner child messages I received were: "I am a bad parent. I am a bad husband. I am bad. Even God thinks so."

. . . .

If God were standing in front of you right now, what would He say? God would say to me, "_____

_____

_____."

God acted and looked like _____

_____

_____

_____

_____

The inner child messages I received were _____

_____

_____

_____

_____

. . . .

If your answers had a negative tone, you may be operating from a negative concept of God. You may have even suffered some form of spiritual abuse. Let's see how we can change these perceptions and maintain a healthy, positive relationship with God.

Our Future Relationship with God

In this section I first want to specifiy how you really feel about God at this very point in your life. Open this exercise with a prayer. Use the following as an example or make up a prayer of your own.

Dear Lord God,

I ask You now to reveal my true feelings to me. I know You won't be alarmed at what my feelings are because you already know them. I trust Your love for me, no matter what I feel for You. I know You will never forsake me. Give me the strength to see my true emotions and feelings toward You. Help me to see any resentments and frustrations I hold against You, because I know these feelings may be blocking Your love and wisdom in my life. I know that only when my true feelings are confessed to You, can You heal me and allow me to have an enhanced relationship with You.

Next, tell God exactly how you really feel. If you're angry, frustrated, or scared, tell Him. If you truly feel deep love and affection for Him, tell Him. Remember, God is interested in our true feelings for Him. It is only by being honest that God can mend us.

Remember Sally Dansen, the woman who learned of a past history of sexual abuse? She wrote her feelings toward God.

"I feel downright angry and confused toward God, even though I know I shouldn't. He let me get hurt as a little child and I don't understand that. I'm mad because He didn't protect me."

If you have experienced physical, sexual, or emotional abuse or neglect, have you ever felt this way toward God? _____ yes _____ no   If you answered no, you are probably still denying. Most individuals who have been harmed have these feelings to some degree.

Now it's your turn.

I feel _____

_____

_____

_____ toward God, because _____

_____

_____

_____

If you had difficulty expressing your feelings to God, try to write Him a letter, pouring out all your feelings. Use the space provided on page 148.

Now, take two chairs into a private room. Face the chairs toward each other. Sit in one and imagine God in the other. Read your letter aloud to Him. If you falter or become afraid, ask Him for strength, then continue.

Another way you could do this exercise is to sit comfortably somewhere and picture the serene place I had you describe in chapter 9. Visualize God sitting next to you in this place and read your letter aloud to Him. Remember

```
┌──────────────────────── ✉ ────────────────────────┐
│                                                     │
│   Dear God,                                         │
│                                                     │
│      I feel _____        │
│                                                     │
│      _____        │
│                                                     │
│      _____        │
│                                                     │
│      _____        │
│                                                     │
│      _____        │
│                                                     │
│      _____        │
│                                                     │
│      _____        │
│                                                     │
│      _____        │
│                                                     │
│                          Yours,                     │
│                                                     │
│                          _____        │
│                                                     │
└─────────────────────────────────────────────────────┘
```

the rules of this place. You must invite Him because God won't come uninvited.

In order to begin building a positive relationship with God, you must first be honest with Him. Our ultimate goal is an intimate, personal relationship with God like we have with no one else. The only way this can occur is by opening up all your feelings to Him. You're not showing Him anything He doesn't already know. God truly knows all our darkest and deepest feelings and thoughts. The Apostle Paul told the early Christians, "And there is no creature hidden from His sight, but all things are naked and open to the eyes of Him to whom we must give account" (Heb. 4:13).

Actually, all you are doing is showing your feelings about God to yourself.

• •

How did you feel after performing this exercise? Be honest. Did you feel silly? Did you feel disrespectful? Both feelings are entirely natural. I felt _____

_____

_____

• •

If you were at all successful at honestly conveying your feelings to Him, you should feel some sort of relief—a weight lifted off your shoulders. God not only sees who we are, He accepts us where we are and loves us as no one else can love us. It doesn't matter what we tell Him or how we feel; His love is unearned and unconditional. What does that mean?

1. God's love for us is *unearned*. It is not based on anything we have done in the past. Nor is it based on anything we can do in the future. There is nothing we can do to make Him want to continue or discontinue this love. It's just there, all the time.
2. God's love for us is *unconditional*. We do not have to do anything to get Him to love us. Further, even if we really mess up and are "bad," God still loves us. God will never stop loving us.

• •

How do you feel about these two aspects of God's love? Have you known them intellectually, but not felt them emotionally? ____ yes ____ no   Why or why not? _____

_____

_____

_____

• •

Through Jesus Christ, God allows us to have a deep personal relationship with Him. In this relationship, we can express ourselves directly to God. "Jesus said to him, 'I am the way, the truth, and the life. No one comes to the Father except through Me'" (John 14:6).

• •

What do you feel makes this relationship like no other in your life? _____

_____

_____

• •

Ways to Build This Relationship

There are three main ways to build this relationship with God: prayer, Scripture study, and church attendance. These won't earn you any extra points with God (His love is unearned), but they will help you maintain a spiritual communion with Him.

Prayer   You have seen that prayer is an integral part of my counseling. Each step my patients take in their inner child work is taken on prayer. God's healing power is released through prayer. Thus, prayer is a necessary tool for an enhanced relationship with God.

• •

Describe your prayer life below. (For example, do you frequently pray for specific things to happen in your life? Do you pray regularly? Do you use prayer as a means of communication with God?)

_____

_____

_____

_____

How do you feel while praying? (For example, do you feel joyful, sorrowful, ashamed, insincere—like you're just going through the motions?) _____

_____

_____

_____

_____

Why do you think you feel this way? (Is it because of your childhood perceptions of God? Do you think you're supposed to feel this way because of church teachings?) _____

_____

_____

_____

How do you perceive your relationship with God—as personal, intimate, distant? _____

_____

_____

• •

Now for this next exercise, think of the last time you prayed to God. When you have that picture in your mind, try and focus on the feelings you felt and list any inner child statements you might have heard during this prayer session.

Bill Johnson was another workaholic I was counseling, using Inner Child therapy. He wrote the following inner child statements he heard over and over during prayer:

> "I'm wasting God's time with my petty problems, there are more severe problems in the world God needs to hear."
>
> "I'm really not worthy of God's time."
>
> "I'm not a good Christian to have all these doubts and feelings about God."

Now list any feelings or inner child statements you've heard during prayer.

_____

_____

_____

_____

_____

_____

_____

_____

For each of your inner child messages, assign the player that is saying them to you. For Bill, we could easily assign the critical parent voice.

How so? Each of his statements had the two telltale characteristics of critical parent voice: irrational and unspecific thoughts. How could Bill become more worthy of God's time? There is no specific way. Is it rational to think Bill isn't a worthy person just because his problems seem minor compared to the world's? No!

Who is the overriding player speaking to you during prayer? _____

Unfortunately, the critical parent (Satan) loves to get to us through prayer. It's the goal of this critical parent voice to undermine our relationship with God.

The voice we want to hear, the one we should hear during prayer is the good parent voice (which is actually the Holy Spirit speaking for God). How else can we receive God's word or answer to our questions? Thus, we need to learn how to substitute this voice for the critical parent voice, which we will do with the following exercise. Preface this exercise with a prayer.

Lord,

     I am having trouble keeping a clear mind. Help me to hear Your voice rather than my critical parent voice. Help me to maintain this voice in my life. I know it is only through the good parent voice that I can receive Your guidance and wisdom in my life. I know that's the key to my happiness, Lord.

This prayer will also help if you ever sit down and find your thoughts wandering from prayer. Don't try to fight your thoughts, just say this prayer, asking God to refocus your mind on the prayer at hand.

Look at the inner child messages you listed above and write out what you think a good parent message would be for each critical parent message below.

For an example, let's look at Bill Johnson's inner child messages.

• •

Critical Parent Message	Good Parent Message
"I'm wasting God's time with my petty problems; there are more severe problems in the world God needs to hear."	"My problems may seem minor, but no problem is too small for God to hear. He is omniscient. He can be everywhere at the same time. There is no limit to his power."
"I'm really not worthy of God's time."	"I am definitely worthy of God's time. He loves me unconditionally. I am just as worthy of His love as anyone else on this earth."

Critical Parent Message	Good Parent Message
"I'm not a good Christian to have all these doubts and feelings about God."	"What is a good Christian anyway? Whose standards do I need to meet? God's, and I've already met those, thanks to Jesus. (See John 3:16.) His love is unconditional. Further, if I show my true feelings to God, then I deepen my intimate relationship with Him, which is what He wants."

• •

Now it's your turn. What critical parent messages do you hear? What do you suppose your counter, good parent message would be?

• •

Critical Parent Message	Good Parent Message
_____	_____
	_____
	_____
_____	_____
	_____
	_____
_____	_____
	_____

• •

If you still find yourself having a difficult time with your prayer relationship with God, consult with your pastor.

Scripture Study   Let me preface this section by saying I have not had formal seminary training nor have I done extensive biblical research. The following information is my opinion, based on my years of professional counseling and my own spiritual awakening.

To best understand Scriptures, they must be examined from several different perspectives. First, the Bible is a storybook about people during a certain time period. It is important to consider the *historical context* of the Bible when quoting passages for present-day application.

First and Second Corinthians, for example, were letters written by the Apostle Paul to the church in Corinth. The historical context of these letters is the city of Corinth, one of the largest centers of commerce in the Roman empire and known for the people's immorality. Thus, when Paul wrote to the Corinthian followers of Christ not to be "unequally yoked" with unbelievers, he was warning the church to remain pure. The heart of the verse applies today—we need to remain pure—but the letter of the verse could be misconstrued, if taken literally, to mean "don't associate with unbelievers." This is *not* the application of the verse, which shows how important taking the verses in their historical context is.

The next point to consider is *your state of mind* while reading the Bible. If you are feeling depressed or anxious, it's easier to interpret the Scriptures as condemning and negative.

The last and most significant point to remember is the *spiritual context* of the Bible. While it is a historical account of a people during earlier times, it is still spiritually inspired by God. Therefore, the Bible has a timeless application. God talks to us through the Scriptures. He loves, corrects, encourages, and instructs us through these words.

Let's do an exercise to see how these points relate.

Read Exodus, chapter 16, in its entirety:

• •

What is the historical context of this chapter? In other words, what happened to the Israelites? _____

_____

_____

_____

_____

How were you feeling while reading this chapter? What was your state
of mind? _____

_____

_____

_____

What is the spiritual intent of this chapter? _____

_____

_____

_____

What application does this chapter have for us today? _____

_____

_____

_____

How is God's love for us demonstrated in this passage? _____

_____

_____

_____

• •

Frequent Bible reading enhances our relationship with God and will, in
turn, enhance our relationship with others. Daily devotional books such as
the Minirth-Meier Serenity Series can help guide your Scripture study into a
productive relationship with God.

For the next week, keep a record of what you are feeling each time you
study a Scripture passage. Write out the passage. Under this, record any inner
child messages you've heard while reading this Bible section. Then next to

each inner child message, write out the player you think is talking to you. If it is the critical parent, quickly ask God to substitute a good parent message and write it next to the critical parent message.

Use the following format for this Scripture study. And if you find it useful, do this whenever you perform any Bible study.

Bible Passage: _____

   While reading this passage, I felt: _____
_____

   My Inner Child messages were: Player who said them:

   _____   _____

   _____   _____

   _____   _____

• •

If you received a critical parent message, what is the corresponding good parent message?

   _____

   _____

   _____

   _____

• •

Church   The third way to enhance and maintain an intimate relationship with God is through church attendance. We can't earn God's love this way, but by exposing ourselves to other believers we gain inspiration for furthering our relationship with God. Church is an excellent forum for worshiping God as well as for being nurtured by Him.

How do you feel in church? (Is it a positive and uplifting experience or a reproachful, shaming experience? Is it primarily a social experience or one you have no feelings about?) _____

_____

_____

_____

What is it about your church that makes you feel good? _____

_____

_____

What is it about your church that makes you feel bad? _____

_____

_____

"I went to church the other Sunday," Sally Dansen commented to me one day.

"Tell me about it. How'd you feel?" I asked.

"It was the same old talk. Men telling me what to do and how to act. I'm thinking about quitting altogether. I actually feel much worse when I go than when I stay home."

Sally's feelings are not that uncommon. Many of us hear a lot of negative messages when we attend church. See if any of the following statements sound familiar to you.

1. ____ Everyone else is dressed nicer than me or my kids.
2. ____ Everyone else 'has it together' more than I do. They are all better Christians than I am.
3. ____ The pastor knows my deepest, darkest sins and is talking directly to me, reproaching me for my uncleanliness.

4. ____ I'm not worthy to be in this church with all of these better, more sincere Christians.
5. ____ This church is full of hypocrites.
6. ____ It doesn't help me to attend church on Sundays; I just continue to sin the rest of the week.
7. ____ I'm too busy to go to church; there are a million other things I need to be doing.
8. ____ I don't need this church to be a good Christian.

• •

Can you think of some more inner child messages you hear while in church or messages that keep you from attending? If so, list them below.

• •

_____

_____

_____

_____

_____

_____

Which player is speaking to you through the messages in this list? _____

• •

If you listed mostly negative messages, such as those in my list, you are hearing your critical parent voice again. However, if you have some positive feelings about church attendance, then you were probably hearing your good parent voice.

For some reason, the critical parent voice is particularly loud in church settings. The critical parent voice loves to disguise itself as spiritual guidance because we are more vulnerable in this area. You will reduce Satan's influence in your church life if you recognize the critical parent's tone.

Let's conclude this chapter with a prayer.

Dear God,

    I need You so much. With so many negative messages assailing me from the critical parent, I need Your constant love and unconditional acceptance. Help me, Lord, to reach out to You through prayer and to learn more about You through Bible readings. Help me to turn my negative perceptions about church into positive ones and to see You, not my own shortcomings. Thank you, Lord, for your unconditional and unearned love.

11

Improving Your Relationship with Yourself

Our second most significant and important relationship is the one with ourselves. Yet, it is frequently the most neglected and abused. In fact, many of us never even conceive of having a relationship with ourselves. But we do.

We engage in constant communication with ourselves; we share opinions with ourselves, both negative and positive, and we constantly tell ourselves what we think of ourselves.

Check the statement below that indicates how you felt the last time you remember failing at an activity. This exercise will help gauge where you stand in your current relationship with yourself.

* *

1. _____ I felt stupid and ignorant. How could I even expect to pass such a difficult test?

2. _____ I felt fine. It was the fault of the person or persons who gave me the activity to do.

3. _____ I felt okay. I tried my best. Next time, I'll try a little harder and maybe do better.

4. _____ I felt okay. Maybe I'm just not meant to do this activity. Everyone is better at some things than others.

* *

How you answered will reflect how you feel about yourself. These feelings will determine how comfortable you are with yourself.

The Uniqueness of This Relationship

Several things set this relationship with ourselves apart from other relationships. First, we are always with ourselves; we never get away. We have the luxury of physically leaving another person when the interchange becomes difficult. Not so with ourselves. We never get away from our self-talk.

Second, we are constantly communicating and interacting with ourselves. Put another way, we are constantly giving negative and positive messages to our inner child. So how do we live with ourselves?

First, if our messages are negative, we have to learn to identify and change this self-talk for the better. Then we have to learn to love ourselves. And to do this, we have to understand our history, which affects the way we treat ourselves.

What Happened to This Relationship?

As with any other relationship, the way you treat yourself is based on what you learned while growing up. I see many patients who have been conditioned to place themselves in a subordinate position. This can cause a problem in your relationship with yourself.

Check the following statements that apply to you.

• •

1. _____ I always take care of my children's emotional needs before my own.
2. _____ When I hear of a friend's or relative's problems, I feel consumed by a need to make things better for them. I sometimes consider myself responsible for their problems.
3. _____ I spend a lot of energy and time worrying about the problems of others around me.

4. _____ I frequently compare myself to others around me in terms of dress, conduct, and appearance, and find myself coming out second to these other people.

5. _____ I frequently feel abandoned and alone if no one is around me to say they love me and to validate me.

6. _____ I require the attention of others to feel worthwhile.

7. _____ I am very uncomfortable when I am alone.

8. _____ The barometer of how I feel about myself changes depending upon how others feel about me.

9. _____ I am not comfortable receiving a compliment. I frequently try to discount it by saying, "You could have easily done as well."

• •

If you could even check one of the above statements, you probably put yourself second to others. There are several reasons we do this.

Cultural Conditioning

Many people, especially women, are conditioned by their upbringing to think of themselves as second to others. Take Ethel, for example. Ethel was raised in a male-dominated household. Her father worked long hours and her mother stayed home, caring for the children. When Ethel's father was home, life revolved around him. He liked having a good cold drink and watching sports after a hard day at the office. Dinner waited until he had finished watching what he wanted. Ethel's mother cooked, served, and cleaned after all the meals, of course.

Ethel's mother planned her schedule according to her husband's. And if he changed his plans to include her, she dropped her own plans to be with him.

Our society is moving away from this being the typical family scenario. But, for a long time, the provider/breadwinner role has been seen as a more important role than the mother/homemaker role, leaving women often treated as second-class citizens.

. . . .

Define what you saw as your parents' roles during your child-hood. What was your father's role? (Was he the breadwinner? The disciplinarian? Were his needs seen as superior to your mother's?)

_____

_____

_____

What was your mother's role as you were growing up? (Was she in charge of the domestic duties or did she work? Did she act as an equal to your father?) _____

_____

_____

What sex are you? _____

Can you see from your answers how your own cultural condi-tioning might contribute to your feelings about yourself? ____ yes ____ no   How? _____

_____

_____

. . . .

Misplaced Spirituality

Scripture teaches us to be humble and to love others as we would love ourselves, placing them above ourselves. Humility is not the same as being inferior to others. Nor does it mean we treat ourselves better than others and look down on them. As an illustration, let's consider Betty.

Betty was raised in a family where mother and father were mutually supportive of their children. She was given the freedom to develop her own value system, and was consistently validated as a person. As a result, she grew into an independent adult with a healthy sense of self-worth and self-esteem. She met and married another independent person.

Early in her marriage, Betty had trouble giving up some of her independence. Her husband was equally stubborn.

Through counseling and a renewed spirituality, Betty learned to be humble. She learned to bow her will to her husband and to others. But she did this from a position of strength, because she knew she was still a complete person inside. Her self-worth was not challenged by compromise. Her own free will allowed her to acquiesce. This is humbleness.

Inferiority is vastly different.

By contrast, Jane grew up in a repressive home. Her father ruled with an iron hand, her mother complied to his every wish. Jane's family attended church regularly. One time Jane was caught whispering in church. After the service, one of the adult congregation members commented to Jane's mother, "Too bad the child doesn't know her place. God certainly knows when a child has made a mistake and He will teach her accordingly."

Jane received a strong message about spirituality at an early age: "If you're a proper Christian, you submit to the rules of the church and those around you." The key word here is *submit*. Jane grew up thinking she wasn't as good as others around her. In her adult life, she threw herself into church activities in a desperate attempt to meet some unknown standard of godliness. Unfortunately, the harder she worked, the worse she felt.

Think back to the spiritual teachings you received as a child. Check the following statements if they reflect your spiritual upbringing.

• •

1. _____ I was taught to refrain from typical childlike behavior (laughter, play, excitement, enthusiasm), especially when attending church or Sunday school.
2. _____ My childhood church was adult-dominated. The children were excluded from the service and allowed to participate only in a nursery or Sunday school setting.
3. _____ I did not enjoy attending church.
4. _____ I always felt on edge and uncomfortable in church, as if everyone around me were watching to make sure I behaved.

5. _____ I felt that God didn't pay much attention to children.
6. _____ The minister never greeted me or called me by name.
7. _____ I looked forward to church and Sunday school every Sunday.
8. _____ I felt wanted and special whenever I went to church.
9. _____ The pastor was a very warm, loving person toward me, always greeting me by name.

• •

If you could check at least one of the first six statements, there is a possibility you were taught to consider yourself inferior based on spiritual teachings. By contrast, if you could check one of statements seven through nine, you may have had a healthy spiritual upbringing and a positive church experience.

Negative Childhood Messages

As I mentioned in the fourth through sixth chapters, the messages our inner child receives are very influential and remain with us as we mature into adulthood. If we received messages of unworthiness, we have probably brought those negative messages into adulthood and may not like ourselves today.

For instance, Billy was born at a difficult time. His family was impoverished. Billy's father worked long hours at two jobs to make ends meet. His mother was mentally incapacitated. From an early age, Billy was forced to take on more responsibility than his maturity warranted. His father had very stringent standards for Billy. His mother went along with his father. Though Billy was taking on more and more responsibilities at home, he was never praised for his home or school accomplishments.

As Billy grew into an adult, he searched desperately for the validation he never received as a child. He always felt others could do better than he did.

Think back once again to your childhood and the inner child messages you may have heard. Were you frequently validated as a person? Did your parents praise you? Did you feel worthy as a person? Look over the following statements. Check those that applied to your situation.

. . . .

1. ____ I can count on one hand the number of times I heard from my mother or father, "I'm proud of you. You did a great job this time."
2. ____ I always felt I never quite achieved the standards my mother or father had for me in school, doing chores, at activities, and even now in my adult life.
3. ____ I was always second best to my brother or sister in my parents' eyes.

. . . .

If you could check at least one of these statements, there is a possibility that you are carrying around inner child messages that say you are inferior to others.

Martyr

There are some people who truly feel they are the victims of society. From these people, you will hear complaints about life such as: "I never receive a fair deal. Everyone else is out to get me." Despite their protests, these people are actually attached to their martyr role.

The classic example is the wife of the alcoholic. She suffers because of her husband's drinking. She protects the children from his drinking and covers for her husband year after year because it's "her lot in life."

. . . .

Was there a martyr in your family that bravely held things together in the face of adversity and suffering? ____ yes ____ no
If so, describe the situation. _____

_____

_____

_____

(If it was a parent, you may try to copy this behavior in your adult life. But understand, we are talking about spouses who seem to relish

their suffering, not spouses who remain in unpleasant situations because of their commitment to the marriage.)

Many martyrs actually feel superior rather than inferior. They feel
they are above the rest of us because they can handle all the pain and
suffering they've been through. In either case, whether the martyr
feels inferior or superior to others, deep inside he or she really
doesn't like herself or himself very much.

• •

Do You Like Yourself?

Answer the following questions as truthfully as possible. We are gauging
how you feel about yourself, so it serves no purpose to be insincere in your
answers. You are only cheating yourself.

1. When I'm alone with nothing to do, I feel _____

_____

_____

2. When I think of asserting myself in a class such as Bible
study, I fear what others will do or think. ____ yes ____ no   Why?

_____

_____

3. When I'm in a room with a lot of people, I tend to _____

_____

_____

4. How much time in a day do you spend completely alone
with no structured activity (excluding sleeping, viewing television,

or listening to music)? ____ seconds ____ minutes ____ hours, or
____ none at all

5. When you're completely alone, do you have the television
or radio on to keep you company? ____ yes ____ no

Look back over your answers. Do you find yourself rarely alone with no activity or diversions? Perhaps you don't like yourself very much. If your answers show a reluctance to assert your thoughts and ideas into conversations, you may not have a positive self-image.

Charlotte Kingsley was thirty-six and single. Her answers to the above questions reflected that she rarely, if ever, was alone. But Charlotte was the envy of everyone in her office and congregation. Here was an attractive, career woman who was willing to help on any church committee. Always vivacious and outgoing, Charlotte was the life of the party. However, she hated going home to an empty house.

On weekends, Charlotte either filled her days with activities or spent much of her time in bed. Charlotte didn't like herself. In fact, she went to great lengths to avoid herself.

Four Ways We Avoid Ourselves

1. Drivenness. Are you a driven person? This seems to be the epidemic (as one form of codependency) for the 90s. A driven person is one who has an insatiable desire to do more and complete more. It's the wife and mother who belongs to five church or social charity committees and is the PTA president. It's the man or woman who works ten or more hours a day at his or her job. It's the pastor who tries to visit every shut-in in the congregation and spends little time at home. It's even the therapist who carries a full patient load and tries to write a book!

Driven behavior is rewarded and applauded by our society. Bosses love driven employees. (Who wouldn't when you can get sixty hours for the price of forty?) By and large, driven people are the success stories in our society.

Do you consider yourself driven? Drivenness is a way we avoid spending time with ourselves. Take the following self-test.

. . . .

List, by day, all the activities you're currently committed to, including your job.

Monday: _____

Tuesday: _____

Wednesday: _____

Thursday: _____

Friday: _____

Saturday: _____

Sunday: _____

Do you have at least one activity other than your job on each day of the week? ____ yes ____no

Do you have more than one activity on any given day other than your job? ____ yes ____ no

Now attach a time estimate to your daily schedule.

a. Note the number of hours you work per day, including travel time.

b. Note the number of hours you spend in all other activities per day, including travel time.

c. Note the number of hours per day you spend doing family chores.

d. Note the number of hours each day you spend in child care responsibilities and/or with your spouse.

e. Note the average number of hours you sleep per night.

f. Add up the total number of hours and subtract from twenty-four. This gives you your total hours of free time.

g. On the average, how many hours a day do you have with no scheduled activities or chores? (Fill in for each day.)

_____ Monday

_____ Tuesday

_____ Wednesday

_____ Thursday

_____ Friday

_____ Saturday

_____ Sunday

Is there free time left over every day of the week? _____ yes _____ no

• •

I performed this exercise myself and found the need for greater balance in my life. So I decided to do something to create this balance on a recent weekend trip I made for the Minirth-Meier Tunnell & Wilson Clinic.

I was to lead a seminar on, ironically, drivenness and workaholism. I had about four hours of unstructured time during the entire weekend. I could have used this time to polish my presentation, prepare more visual aids, or attend other seminars. And, indeed, if I had done this, I would have had a better presentation, no doubt about it.

Instead, I chose to drive to the ocean and just sit and watch the waves. Time. I gave myself crucial time to just be alone.

How about you? I don't want to present a right or wrong answer to the above exercise. You have to decide if you have enough time in your day or week for just yourself. It has to be unstructured. Time to just be, to enjoy being alive, to be with you.

• •

How much time do you have to do this, based on your answers to the above exercise? _____

Are you satisfied with this amount of time? _____ yes _____ no   If not, what of the listed activities can you give up? _____

_____

_____

_____

• •

Remember you are not indispensable; you have limits and God wants you to use them. You can say no and still be a worthy person.

My advice to workaholics and driven people is to achieve a balance in their lives. Schedule time to just be by yourself, at least some time each day. And be selfish about this time. Your job will come and go, ultimately even your family may come and go, but you will always be with yourself and if you forsake this person, what is left? All the other relationships in your life will suffer.

For more insight on how to recognize and treat driven behavior, I recommend the book *We Are Driven* by Dr. Robert Hemfelt, Dr. Frank Minirth, and Dr. Paul Meier.

2. Codependency. Also prevalent in today's world, codependent behavior blocks any positive relationship with yourself as well as others. But what is codependency?

For our purposes, codependency is a relationship problem—dependent people trying to get their needs met through relationships with others. They are the ".5 persons" I spoke of earlier.

I am not going to go into much depth on codependency since several excellent recovery books already do that. I especially recommend *Love Is a Choice* by Dr. Robert Hemfelt, Dr. Frank Minirth and Dr. Paul Meier and the *Love Is a Choice Workbook* by these same authors and Dr. Deborah Newman and Dr. Brian Newman.

Codependent behavior is a way to block a positive relationship with yourself because you are constantly looking to others for validation of your self-worth. The codependent person will seek approval at all costs and do whatever is necessary to keep others pleased. Almost like a chameleon, the codependent will change to meet whatever the environment warrants.

Just as we are all driven to some extent, so are we all codependent to some extent. We want others to like us. The difference comes from the degree we let this behavior control our lives and our relationships.

Take the following self-test to see how much codependency may be controlling your life. Check those statements that apply to your actions or behaviors.

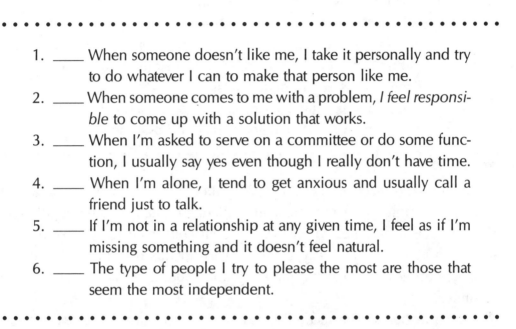

• •

1. ____ When someone doesn't like me, I take it personally and try to do whatever I can to make that person like me.

2. ____ When someone comes to me with a problem, *I feel responsible* to come up with a solution that works.

3. ____ When I'm asked to serve on a committee or do some function, I usually say yes even though I really don't have time.

4. ____ When I'm alone, I tend to get anxious and usually call a friend just to talk.

5. ____ If I'm not in a relationship at any given time, I feel as if I'm missing something and it doesn't feel natural.

6. ____ The type of people I try to please the most are those that seem the most independent.

• •

If you could check at least one of these statements, you may have codependent tendencies. If you are concerned, again I refer you to *Love Is a Choice* and the *Love Is a Choice Workbook*. For the purpose of this workbook, be aware that your codependent behavior may be blocking a positive relationship with yourself.

3. Substance abuse. Physiologically, drugs and alcohol numb or block your body's natural mental functioning. They also anesthetize your emotions and keep you distant from your feelings and a relationship with yourself. This is exactly what your inner child does not want. The inner child wants you to feel and heal the pain he or she is carrying.

See if you are using alcohol or drugs to avoid facing your inner emotions.

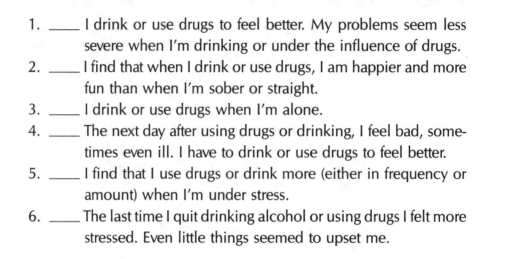

1. _____ I drink or use drugs to feel better. My problems seem less severe when I'm drinking or under the influence of drugs.
2. _____ I find that when I drink or use drugs, I am happier and more fun than when I'm sober or straight.
3. _____ I drink or use drugs when I'm alone.
4. _____ The next day after using drugs or drinking, I feel bad, sometimes even ill. I have to drink or use drugs to feel better.
5. _____ I find that I use drugs or drink more (either in frequency or amount) when I'm under stress.
6. _____ The last time I quit drinking alcohol or using drugs I felt more stressed. Even little things seemed to upset me.

If you could check even just one of the above statements, substance abuse may be preventing you from seeing and relating to the real you. I highly recommend you seek help from a professional counselor for any substance abuse. No matter how hard you might work in this workbook, if you use alcohol or drugs to avoid feeling your emotions, your inner child will never be reclaimed.

4. Perfectionism. Perfectionism is a way we avoid a positive relationship with ourselves because we unconsciously feel we must do everything perfectly to be a worthy person. This standard is not only unreal, it's never going to be obtained because God created us as human beings, which means He allows us to make mistakes so we can learn. Only by allowing yourself the freedom to make mistakes can you accept your inner child as it is, faults and all.

Perfectionism is a very subtle way to block a positive relationship with yourself. The premise of perfectionism is that if we can control the environment around us, we will be okay. Thus, it actually perpetuates denial. We don't have to face our emotions or problems if we put our energy into controlling the environment.

The problem is, you can never control your environment. It is in a state of constant flux. So, what happens is a frantic attempt for this control, which is evidenced by doing tasks over and over again.

Are you in this vicious cycle? Check the following statements that apply to you:

. . . .

1. ____ I rarely am able to do a task once and leave it alone.
2. ____ I find that being average is unacceptable.
3. ____ When I have tried to force myself not to engage in perfection-istic behaviors, I find that I feel uneasy and uncomfortable.
4. ____ To settle for not being perfect is to be unworthy in God's eyes.

Could you check one of the above statements? If so, was your perfectionism learned as a child from a role model? Or, has it developed in your adult life to make up for what you perceive are your inadequacies? _____

_____

_____

. . . .

Each of these behaviors will block any lasting relationship with yourself. And, without a relationship with yourself, you have little chance of maintaining a positive relationship with others. Why?

Primarily because the way you feel about yourself is unconsciously transmitted in your actions and modeling behavior toward others. Remember these are the two best ways we learn and communicate with others. The spoken word is the least effective. So if you feel inferior or uncomfortable with yourself, others will pick this up unconsciously and they may even treat you this way in return.

Thus, the next step in shoring up your relationships is to reestablish a positive relationship with yourself. It was there when you were born, put in by God. Now is the time to rediscover it.

Reestablishing a Relationship with Yourself

Perform the following exercises when you have time to be totally alone and uninterrupted.

• •

1. In the blanks below, write out all the traits you like about yourself (talents, accomplishments, strengths). Try to think of at least ten.

Things I Like About Myself:

1. _____
2. _____
3. _____
4. _____
5. _____
6. _____
7. _____
8. _____
9. _____
10. _____

• •

How'd you do? Have trouble coming up with ten? Most of us do, it's very hard to focus on our strengths. If you couldn't list at least five, go back and reread the first part of this chapter. Are there any blockages working in you? If so, ask God to remove them and try this exercise again.

• •

2. Now list what you feel are your shortcomings. Try to come up with at least ten and list them below.

Things I Don't Like About Myself:

1. _____

2. _____

3. _____

4. _____

5. _____

6. _____

7. _____

8. _____

9. _____

10. _____

• •

You probably had no problem coming up with this list. Most of us have a good idea what our faults are. Now to be sure this isn't the critical parent voice speaking to us, give each of these shortcomings the critical parent test:

a. Are they rational?

b. Can they be fixed?

Examples of valid shortcomings are: I'm impatient, irritable, or egotistical. An example of an invalid shortcoming and a critical parent message is: I'm not a good parent, good Christian, or good person. Invalid shortcomings do not possess measurable means to improve.

By contrast, if impatience is a shortcoming, there are ways to improve this. You could use techniques such as deep breathing and counting to overcome your impatience. You could also read some books or listen to tapes of soft, relaxing music.

• •

3. Now go back and cross off any invalid shortcomings or critical parent messages you wrote in number two.

4. Confess your valid shortcomings to God and ask for His forgiveness *and* for His strength to help you overcome them.

5. Go into the bathroom or another room with a mirror. Stand

facing the mirror. Read aloud your shortcomings list. After each short-coming, forgive yourself for this.

For example, "Self, I forgive you for being irritable."

6. After forgiving yourself for your shortcomings, read the positive traits list. After each positive trait, reinforce how proud you are of yourself.

For example, "Self, I know you are sympathetic and empathetic to the suffering of others and I am proud of you for this trait."

7. Now read aloud to yourself the following statement in the mirror:

"All I can be is human, therefore I will fall short and make mistakes. I will have weaknesses and I will fail sometimes. But that's okay. I'm only human; I'm not meant to be perfect. I promise to work with God to improve my shortcomings. And I rejoice in my positive traits. I will work with God to enhance and improve these positive traits. But more than anything I love myself and I love my inner child. My inner child is precious, significant, and created by God in His image. I accept myself and my inner child as the Lord accepts me—unconditionally."

8. Close your conversation with yourself by reading the following:

"I accept me totally and unconditionally with all my faults and shortcomings. I will try to see me as God sees me. I will try not to demean myself, but uplift myself. I will focus on my positive traits rather than on my shortcomings. I will use my shortcomings as a way to seek God's guidance and instruction in my life. I will never be perfect, but I will love myself as I am."

9. Close this exercise with a prayer, thanking God for creating you and giving you life.

• •

Reminders

• •

We need our adult voice to reflect the good parent messages in order to protect and nurture our inner child and help this relationship with ourselves prosper. To bring out this adult voice in your everyday life, take two 3 x 5 index cards and print the following messages. Hereafter, carry these cards with you and look at them whenever you are feeling down on yourself.

First Card:

I am a child of God and therefore loved by God. I am created in His image. God will never leave me no matter what happens or what I am thinking. I will not deny my feelings when they come. I will recognize them.

Second Card:

At times my inner child will need to be protected by my good parent (the Holy Spirit). The good parent will protect the inner child and the adult voice will carry out the interaction. But the adult voice will never forsake my inner child. I will not deny the existence of my inner child. I will not believe the lies the critical parent may tell my inner child. I will always call upon the good parent voice to combat the critical parent messages.

• •

Step Eight

Improving Your Relationship with Your Spouse

12

As we begin this section of the workbook, we will discuss the characteristics of a family. Each family is a system of functioning, or dysfunctioning, individuals. There are specific characteristics common to all family systems.

1. *A family is a closed system.* Outside influences that threaten the integrity of the family unit are avoided. Thus, a new son-in-law may not be quickly included into his wife's family. Interestingly, the more dysfunctional the family unit, the more reluctant it is to include newcomers. There is an unwritten code that no one in the unit shares family secrets (such as incest or abuse) with outsiders.

A relatively healthy unit, on the other hand, is more adaptable to new members and more open to sharing information about the unit with outsiders.

2. *Each family member has a role to perform within the family unit.* Every family member inherits a particular role in the family. I'm not talking about breadwinner, housekeeper, or other job assignments. The word *roles*, here, means expected behaviors.

For example, one child may inherit the role of "troublemaker" or "scapegoat" while another may inherit the "model child" role. In unhealthy situations, a child may "parent" one of the parents or become a "peacekeeper" to argumentative parents. One parent might be the "disciplinarian" while the other is the "good guy" or "friend" to the kids.

Each person's role in the family unit is dependent upon all the other members of the unit carrying out their roles. If one person decides to change one's role, the result is chaos in the unit until equilibrium is again found.

3. *Each family unit is governed by written and unwritten rules of conduct.* These rules keep the family unit intact and functioning. They range from where individuals sit at the dinner table to defining proper dress. Some families have regular family meetings to discuss family business. Other families meet only during crises to reinforce proper family conduct and rules and to deal with the stressors at hand.

Any attempt to change the rules of conduct within a family is seriously hampered by the very nature of family dynamics. The more dysfunctional the family system, the less likely it is to bend the rules of conduct.

4. *Being a closed system, when something happens to one part of the family, the rest of the family is affected and will fight to regain its former equilibrium.* Put succinctly, families resist change. It is precisely this characteristic of family systems that has largely refocused psychotherapy from individual counseling to family counseling. I have had many a patient who reclaimed his or her inner child only to return to a dysfunctional family system and again lose touch with that inner child.

Healthy family systems will adapt to change much more quickly than less functional families, but they will all resist it to some degree or another.

With this knowledge in hand, let's begin to discuss the ways to improve relationships within your family. In this chapter and the next few, I will cover the relationships with your current family (spouse and children) as well as your family of origin (parents and siblings).

. . . .

YOUR CURRENT FAMILY

To begin this section, I want you to take an inventory of what your current family system looks like. In the large vacant house provided below, draw a circle for every member in your family. The size of the circle should relate to the relative prominence of that person in the family. And the placement of the circle should relate to where the most interactions (positive and negative) occur.

For example, if your wife and your daughter are frequently engaged in conflict, their two circles should be almost touching. Conversely, if you and your daughter rarely interact, those two circles would be fairly far apart. If you feel you all relate on an equal basis, place all circles an equal distance apart. Then, to each circle, assign roles: Model Child; Troublemaker Child/Scapegoat; Disciplinarian/ Authoritarian Parent; Nurturer Parent; Friend/Playmate Parent; Child-Parent; Peacemaker.

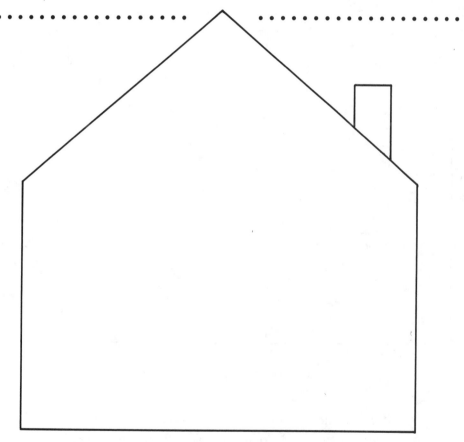

My Family Sculpture

Don't worry if you don't have a role for every family member. You may not be able to discern what roles you and your spouse play or the roles your children play. That's okay for now. The diagram will still be of benefit.

However, if you could assign roles, at least two out of the above list should be present in your family. If you have more than two children, usually there's just one model child and one troublemaker. The other children fall somewhere in between.

I asked Sally Dansen to sculpt her family and family roles. Her completed sculpture looked like the following.

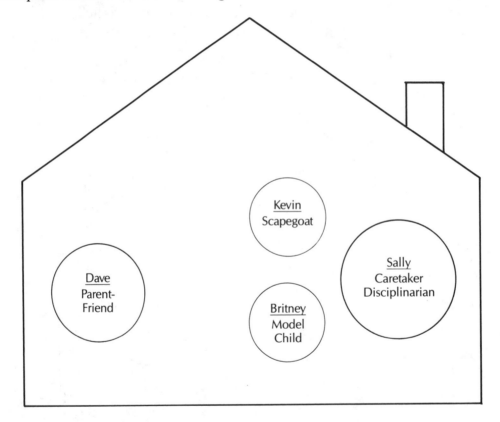

Sally Dansen's Family Sculpture

As you can see, her two children were clustered around her. Her husband, Dave, seemed to stand off to one side. This showed some sort of unhealthy enmeshment between the kids and Sally. Dave, her husband, had either been pushed away because of this enmeshment or was non-participatory in Sally's eyes.

• •

Do you have your family sculpture and roles defined? Good. Take a moment to look at your diagram. What strikes you? _____

_____

_____

Is it a workable system? ____ yes ____ no   What do you think needs to be changed? _____

_____

_____

How easily would the rest of your family accept this change?

_____

_____

_____

• •

While the family may fight your change, the key is to maintain your change until a new equilibrium is reached in the family system. If you are unable to maintain during the fight, things will eventually fall back into the established pattern you diagramed.

Let's see how you can change by using your inner child knowledge. There are two main categories of relationships you enter into in your family: your spouse and your children. In this chapter, I'll cover the relationship with your spouse, and the next chapter, your children.

Relationship with Your Spouse

This relationship is the most tested relationship, other than the one with your own self, since you are physically with your spouse more than any other human being. It is the only human relationship that experiences the unique closeness and intimacy of a sexual relationship. And it is the relationship that may produce offspring connecting you with your spouse for the rest of your children's lives.

As with anything else, your marriage will be greatly influenced by your upbringing. For a female, a marriage will be the most significant relationship she will have with a male other than her father. For a male, marriage will be the most significant relationship he will have with a female other than his mother.

It's exactly this characteristic that makes us tend to marry spouses who resemble our mothers (if we're male) or our fathers (if we're female). We select mates based on our relationship with our opposite sex parent. And we will either marry someone very like, or dislike, our opposite sex parent.

Sages purport, "There are four persons in a marriage: the husband, wife, husband's mother, and wife's father." This fact has been proven over and over in marital counseling.

After the honeymoon, at least two realizations sink in:

1. My spouse is not my daddy (or mommy) and cannot fulfill my needs from my opposite sex parent (although we may go on unconsciously expecting this).

2. My spouse is not what I expected.

I've already discussed the reason for the first realization. The second comes from television, magazines, books, and the movies, which support the "Happily Ever After" phenomenon. It's promised to every couple and when a marriage doesn't turn out so perfectly, people are thrown for a loop.

I will not go into much more detail on the aspects of marriage. For these purposes, I refer you to the Passages of Marriage series by Dr. Frank and Mary Alice Minirth, Dr. Robert and Susan Hemfelt, and Drs. Brian and Deborah Newman.

Here, I want to show how critical parent messages can actually be detrimental to your marriage. To do that, we first have to identify them.

• •

MESSAGES YOUR INNER CHILD IS RECEIVING
FROM YOUR MARRIAGE

Answer the following questions. Be as honest as possible. You might want to preface this exercise with a prayer, asking God to give you the vision you need to see things clearly.

1. How do you feel about your current relationship? (For example, "I feel comfortable with my marriage. I love my spouse as much or more than the day we were married," or "I don't feel the passion I did at the beginning of our marriage. Things have gotten too routine. There's no excitement. My husband and I act more like roommates than lovers.")

_____

_____

_____

_____

2. How would you describe this current relationship? (For example, "We have a working relationship. I have my role and so does my husband, but we rarely talk anymore except about daily routines and the kids.") _____

_____

_____

_____

_____

3. What do you see as the strengths? (For example, "We get along very well. I can tell my wife anything. She is my best friend.") _____

_____

_____

_____

_____

4. What do you see as the weaknesses? (For example, "We never

talk—really communicate. We make too many assumptions about how the other person is feeling.")

_____

_____

_____

_____

_____

5. Does your husband or wife share your perceptions? What would be his or her answers to the above questions?

1. _____

_____

_____

2. _____

_____

_____

3. _____

_____

_____

4. _____

_____

_____

6. For the next week, I want you to keep a daily journal. In this journal record the actual events or incidents that happen between you and your spouse. Next to each incident, write out your emotional response and feelings, being as specific as possible.

For example, "My husband came home at 8:30 P.M. over three hours late, without calling today. I felt angry and resentful. I felt hurt because he didn't care enough about me to even call."

Or, "My wife surprised me with a candlelit dinner for two and sent the kids to a neighbor's. I felt cherished and loved. I felt fortunate to have her in my life."

7. At the end of the week you should have a list of events and a list of feelings based on the events. Beside each emotional response, see if you can write out an inner child message you might be receiving.

• •

For our first incident above, the inner child message would be "I don't matter. I feel abandoned by my husband."

Don't discount feelings you have when your mate is unresponsive. Silence is a very powerful communicator to the inner child. In fact it can sometimes be even more detrimental than the spoken word. The messages your inner child receives from silence or being ignored by your spouse include:

• You don't count. You don't matter enough to even talk to;
• You're too bad for me to communicate with;
• You have made me so mad, I can't even discuss it with you.

In addition to silence, insincere behaviors can produce these same inner child messages. For example, if you're angry at your spouse and maybe not even conscious of it, you might speak to him or her cordially, even politely. However, your words won't reflect your feelings or actions and your spouse will pick up on your behaviors. He or she will know you're unhappy simply by the way you're acting.

So while keeping your journal, be sure to include silence or being ignored by your spouse as well as any times you felt he or she treated you insincerely.

• •

8. Now peruse your journal. What were your feelings this week about your marriage? (For example, were you angry, sad, unhappy, happy, joyful?) _____

_____

_____

_____

_____

If you found out that you were unhappy, sad, or angry most of this week in your marriage, what would you like to see improved in this relationship? (For example, "I'd like my husband to communicate better with me. Tell me what he's feeling and be open to hearing how I feel. I'd like this on a daily basis.") _____

_____

_____

_____

• •

Marital problems are only another symptom of a hurt or wounded inner child in either or both spouses. However, this relationship is important enough to your well-being that it may behoove you to seek marital counseling. When I see a couple, I will usually concentrate on the simplest marital problem first, the one that seems most easily fixed. From this point, I work with the couple to gradually more serious problems.

• •

Do you see a marital problem that you would like to see resolved? ____ yes ____ no   If yes, what is the problem? (For example, "We don't communicate very well.")

_____

_____

_____

• •

Well over 80 percent of the marriage problems I see in my professional practice have to do with husbands not communicating with their wives. This is so prevalent that there are now many books written about male/female communication. *The Language of Love* by Gary Smalley and John Trent is one good source.

Males and females typically communicate from two different parts of their brain. Males tend to use words to transmit and receive information. Females tend to use words to transmit feelings. Males, typically, are uncomfortable talking about feelings; they prefer to show them through actions or behaviors. Females, typically, desire to hear feelings in words and will interpret an absence of words as a negative message. ("He won't tell me how he feels; therefore he must not love me.")

• •

Looking back over your log of the past week, what behaviors recur, causing the same or similar feelings within you? (For example, he comes home late frequently. I feel angry and hurt.) _____

_____

_____

What messages do you think your inner child receives from these behaviors? (For example, if your husband doesn't call when he's going to be late, your inner child message might be that you're insignificant to him, you're unworthy of the time for a phone call, and your unlovable to him.) The messages to my inner child might be _____

_____

_____

_____

_____

Have you confronted your spouse with this problem? ____ yes ____ no   If so, what was his or her response? (Did he or she admit he or she was wrong and apologize? Or, did he or she look at you like you were crazy?) _____

_____

_____

If not, why haven't you mentioned that his or her behavior bothers you? _____

_____

_____

If you mentioned the problem to your spouse and he or she didn't understand or acknowledge your feelings, you received another powerful message to your inner child. What do you think it was?

_____

_____

_____

It probably was something like: "You're stupid and crazy. You really don't know what you're talking about. You shouldn't have these feelings, they are not valid."

Now look carefully at the inner child messages you wrote above. Examine the tone of the statements, the language, and the nature of what is being said. Is it judgmental or critical? Which player do you think is speaking to your inner child in these instances?

_____

• •

You're correct if you put the critical parent. That voice again, speaking to us as a reaction to what our spouses do. It's easy to see how this can create such conflict in a marriage. The critical parent voice seeks to destroy your happiness and your marriage and it will do whatever it can to accomplish this. *Never doubt that the critical parent is your enemy!*

For every inner child message you wrote in your journal, identify if it is a critical parent voice. If it is, substitute a corresponding good parent message. If not, and if you truly come up with good parent messages, carry through the solution with God's help. Keep in mind the following points which will help your good parent voice be heard.

Point 1: Males and females communicate with different perspectives. The message that comes to the inner child may not be the message the other party meant to send.

Point 2: God created males and females physically, mentally, and emotionally different. He instituted the marriage system so that these differences would complement. It's normal for males and females to be different.

Before we call upon the good parent voice to combat critical parent messages, we should begin with a prayer. You can use the following as a guide if you wish.

Lord,

I acknowledge that You created marriage. For whatever reason, my husband (or wife) and I are currently married and committed to each other. Lord, You have the wisdom and the vision to show how this marriage can work. I ask for Your help now in understanding my partner. Grant me insight, Lord, into what makes him or her do what he or she does. Help me to better understand my spouse. I know, as human beings, my partner and I will fall short and make mistakes. I pray that Your Holy Spirit will make Himself known to me now as I try to hear my good parent voice. Give me the truth and wisdom I need to hear things as they really are.

Thank you, Lord.

Cross out the critical parent messages to your inner child you wrote in your journal or this workbook. Next to these crossed-out statements, write a corresponding good parent message.

For an illustrated example of this, consider Joyce and Steve Johnson. They've been married three years and have no children. Joyce has a good part-time job and Steve has a very demanding mid-level management job. Their first year of marriage was great. They did lots of things together, took long walks, held hands. Joyce was blissfully happy.

But shortly after their one-year anniversary, Steve started to change in Joyce's eyes. He didn't talk to her as much, and he spent most of his time at home reading the paper or watching television.

"Why don't you ever talk to me anymore?" Joyce asked him one evening.

"What are you talking about?" he responded.

"We never talk. We never spend time doing anything together."

"What are you talking about? I'm here every night with you. What else do you want?"

Eventually the situation got so bad they entered counseling with me. Joyce's journal entries looked like the following:

"Monday, October 5th:

Another night of Steve coming home and planting himself on the couch with the game and the newspaper. I asked him if we could talk a little, spend some time together. He invited me to join him watching the game. I got really angry and left the room. My inner child messages might have been: I'm not significant enough to him for him to turn off the game or put down the paper."

After Joyce had learned to call on her good parent voice, she was able to substitute this statement to her inner child:

"The truth is that Steve is a male. He communicates with me differently. He may not be meaning this message at all. I'm free to ask him if the game or the paper really does mean more to him than me. The fact that he's ignoring me does not necessarily mean he doesn't love me.

"I am still worthwhile and significant regardless of how I'm viewing Steve's love. God loves me and will never leave me. I am not responsible for Steve's actions. I am only responsible for how I perceive his actions. Further I can try to talk to him if this behavior continues to bother me. I can read books or seek counseling to help me in my marriage."

As any muscle will be sore when you first start to work out, so you will be a little sore as you begin substituting critical parent messages with good parent statements. This is only natural, since you've been programmed to listen to the critical parent voice all your life. With consistent workouts, that soreness soon ceases. So with continued journaling and objective analysis of your emotional responses to your spouse, you will learn to hear the good parent voice. To accomplish this, I recommend daily journaling for at least the next month.

There's one final step in this relationship with your spouse—forgive yourself and your spouse. For each behavior that you've listed in your journal that bothers you or has caused problems, forgive your spouse (not necessarily to his or her face, but symbolically). Remember forgiving does not mean that the acts were right, it just means that you choose not to hold a grudge against him or her for these acts. Forgiveness will certainly help your marriage, but it will not solve the problems. You still need to actively pursue the corrections to any problems.

13

Step Nine

Improving Your Relationships with Your Children

"Kevin!" Sally yelled. "Leave Britney alone."

"I don't know what to do with that kid. He loves to torment his little sister. Sometimes I think he likes to make her cry," she told her husband, Dave.

"Mmmmm," Dave mumbled as he read the newspaper. "I guess they're just typical kids. Brothers and sisters fight, you know."

"Yeah, but Kevin is always the instigator." Just then Sally saw Kevin hit Britney. Britney started crying and headed for Mom.

"Kevinnnnn!" Sally screamed. "Come here this instant. I warned you!"

She sent Kevin to his room and soothed Britney with a video on the television. "That boy! It's almost like he enjoys getting into trouble," she said to Dave.

Relationships with Your children

The relationship with your kids is like no other relationship on earth, because it is ever changing. For a brief moment, the kids are totally dependent on you; you are God to them. Then as they grow and mature, you become a model for them to learn from. And finally, once they are independent adults, you become a friend to them. Finally, in your old age, you may become physically dependent on them.

There are two very important aspects to consider with this relationship. The first concerns how your inner child is affected by your children's behavior. The second is how your behavior affects the inner child of each of your children. Since this workbook is meant for your recovery and maintenance, I will focus exclusively on the first aspect.

However, as children learn best by modeling, if you recognize and validate your own inner child, you will teach them to do likewise. In addition, if you are operating from the viewpoint of protecting your own inner child, you will be operating from the best parenting posture—the one the Lord wants us to strive for, the good parent model.

• •

AN INVENTORY

First, you need to make a list of all your children as Sally Dansen has done.

| Kevin David Dansen | 10 years old |
| Britney Marie Dansen | 8 years old |

List all your children and their ages below.

Child's Name	Age
_____	_____
_____	_____
_____	_____
_____	_____
_____	_____

• •

Now take each child separately and describe your relationship with him or her. Is it comfortable? Is it conflict-ridden? What are the problems with this relationship? What are the ways you want to improve this relationship? Have you unconsciously assigned this child a role in the family unit (model child, troublemaker, peacemaker between warring adults, child-parent)?

Sally did this. Her descriptions follow.

Child's Name: Kevin

Description of current relationship: Conflict-ridden.
Kevin and I are constantly fighting. I have to be on him all the time to get him to behave. He's always pushing me, always trying to get away with something.

Assigned role of this child in the family unit: I guess I've assigned him the troublemaker role. He sure seems to play that role the most.

Problems with the relationship: Most of the time I have to be on Kevin's case. I yell and scream too much. I feel that I'm always punishing him. And what's worse, Kevin seems to be intensely jealous of his sister, Britney.

Ways I want to improve the relationship: I'd like to have a more peaceful relationship with Kevin. Do things together without having to constantly remind him to behave. Kevin is almost a teenager now. I really want to improve this relationship before he reaches that age.

Child's Name: Britney

Description of current relationship: Britney's my friend.
She and I have a compatible relationship. Oh sure, she gets into trouble, but not as much as Kevin. She seems to want to please her mom. Britney does well in school and enjoys helping me with the household chores.

Assigned role of this child in family unit: I suppose Britney would be the model child.

Problems with the relationship: The only problem I can see is that Britney is more attached to me than I like her to be. I sometimes wonder if she excels at school or home just to please me.

Ways I want to improve the relationship: I guess I'd like to see Britney become more independent—do things more on her own. I'd like Britney to do well in her activities because she wants to not because I want her to.

• •

Now you fill in the following charts for your own children. Include any stepchildren who are or who have lived with you. Don't worry if you can't assign a family role to a child; simply leave that space blank and fill in the rest of the chart. I've provided enough charts for four children. If you have more than four, photocopy the last chart and use the copies for your other children.

• •

Child's Name: _____

Description of current relationship: _____

_____

_____

_____

_____

_____

Assigned role of this child in the family unit:

_____

Problems with the relationship: _____

_____

_____

_____

_____

Ways I want to improve the relationship: _____

_____

_____

_____

_____

Child's Name: _____

Description of current relationship: _____

_____

_____

_____

_____

_____

Assigned role of this child in the family unit:

_____

Problems with the relationship: _____

_____

_____

_____

_____

_____

Ways I want to improve the relationship: _____

_____

_____

_____

_____

Child's Name: _____

Description of current relationship: _____

_____

_____

_____

_____

Assigned role of this child in the family unit:

_____

Problems with the relationship: _____

_____

_____

_____

_____

Ways I want to improve the relationship: _____

_____

_____

Child's Name: _____

    Description of current relationship: _____

_____

_____

_____

_____

_____

_____

    Assigned role of this child in the family unit:

_____

    Problems with the relationship: _____

_____

_____

_____

_____

_____

    Ways I want to improve the relationship: _____

_____

_____

_____

A Relationship Journal

John went beyond the charts. He kept a journal on each of his two children. One week it was on Amanda, age two, the next on Jonathan, age six. One of John's entries on Amanda is below.

> "Saturday, April 15th:
>
>> Child's Name: Amanda
>> Incident: Took Amanda to the store. Big mistake. She saw a stuffed dalmation puppy and demanded I buy it. I said no. She kept asking. I got madder and yelled at her. Amanda started crying and throwing a fit. Eventually, I dragged her out of the store and spanked her. We went home a very unhappy pair.
>>
>> My emotional response: I felt mad and frustrated at the same time. No matter what I did, she wouldn't listen. I couldn't reason with her. I couldn't keep Amanda under control in public. And I even lost my cool with her and physically hurt her when I was angry. I felt inadequate as a parent. The onlookers didn't help.
>>
>> My inner child messages may be: "I am not a very good parent. I'm bad and inadequate and others know it."

By far, you will hear some of the strongest inner child messages when your young children act up. It's natural for young children to act up, sometimes they have to rebel to learn. A rebellious child will invoke a critical parent response every time. It's a fact of life. This makes the business of substituting good parent messages for critical parent messages extra difficult.

If your children have left home, think of the most recent encounter you had with them that wasn't exactly comfortable. Recall what happened and write it down in the following charts. Don't forget to put down silence or no response as an event that invokes a response in you. Ellen, the seventy-year-old widow, lost contact with her only son. She received very powerful inner child messages when her son refused to answer her letters or phone calls.

Let's look at Ellen's account.

Child's Name: Timothy

    Incident: Timothy has just severed all communication with me. He doesn't want me to call or visit him. He won't return my calls and won't answer my letters.

    Emotional responses: 1. Remorse—Did I do something to cause Timothy to leave and to be so unhappy? 2. Anger—How could he treat me like this? I'm his mother. 3. Guilt—If only I'd been a better parent, this wouldn't have happened. 4. Hurt—I am devastated by this abandonment.

    My inner child messages might be: I'm a bad parent. I'm a bad person. I'm not significant enough to communicate with.

I now want you to keep a journal on each of your children—one week per child. In your journal write down every incident that invokes an emotional response as you relate to this particular child. Write down both the incident and what your feelings were. At the end of the week, write out what inner child messages you may be hearing as a result of these incidents. Do this in the blanks provided below. Make sure you also do an account for every child no longer living with you.

Journal Record

Child's Name: _____

Incident: _____

_____

_____

_____

_____

_____

_____

_____

_____

_____

My emotional response: _____

_____

_____

_____

_____

_____

My inner child messages might be:_____

_____

_____

_____

_____

Child's Name: _____

Incident: _____

_____

_____

_____

_____

_____

_____

_____

_____

_____

My emotional response: _____

_____

_____

_____

_____

_____

_____

My inner child messages might be:_____

_____

_____

_____

_____

Child's Name: _____

Incident: _____

_____

_____

_____

_____

_____

_____

_____

_____

_____

My emotional response: _____

_____

_____

_____

_____

_____

My inner child messages might be:_____

_____

_____

_____

_____

Child's Name: _____

Incident: _____

_____

_____

_____

_____

_____

_____

_____

_____

_____

My emotional response: _____

_____

_____

_____

_____

_____

_____

My inner child messages might be:_____

_____

_____

_____

_____

Now I don't expect you to be as specific as Ellen was at this point in the workbook. But I mentioned this illustration so you can see how to channel your thinking in this direction. Ellen had been through months of Inner Child therapy and was ready to hear her good parent voice.

Calling Up the Good Parent

The next task for both John and Ellen was to substitute critical parent inner child messages with good parent messages. Before you go on to do these substitutions, consider the following points.

1. You were a child of God and a human being long before you were a parent. You were okay before children came along and you are still okay. You have made mistakes as a parent because you are

human. Further, God stands ready to forgive you for those mistakes. You did the best parenting you could with what you knew. When your children reach adulthood, regardless of what parenting you gave them, their lives will be their own responsibility.

2. Your happiness and validation do not hinge on your children's actions or behaviors.

3. You can make yourself available in a relationship with your children. You are free to admit the parenting mistakes you made. Their response, or lack of response, does not affect your self-worth.

John and Ellen used these points in arriving at their good parent messages.

John's good parent message was: "I'm a human being. I'm a good person in God's eyes. I make mistakes, and I learn from those mistakes. My self-worth as a parent is never in question in God's eyes and it should not be in mine."

Ellen's was: "It's okay to have these feelings. My emotional responses are part of me. I am a worthy person in God's eyes. Whether Timothy chooses to validate me or not has no bearing on my self-worth. God knows all my faults and He still accepts me and loves me. I know I made some mistakes with Timothy. I've asked for his and for God's forgiveness. Whether Timothy responds or not is completely up to him. I can feel sad about losing a relationship with him and I can feel angry. Both feelings are okay, but I need not blame myself. I did the best job I could as a mother. Now as an adult, Timothy's life and health are under his control, not mine."

Now for each record you made of your relationship with each of your children, write a corresponding good parent message to counter the critical parent message.

• •

Child's Name: _____

Corresponding good parent message: _____

_____

_____

_____

_____

Child's Name: _____

Corresponding good parent message: _____

_____

_____

_____

_____

Child's Name: _____

Corresponding good parent message: _____

_____

_____

_____

_____

• •

When Sally Dansen started replacing her critical parent messages with good parent messages, she found her relationships with both Kevin and Britney improved. As she started to recognize and validate her inner child, Sally became less enmeshed with her children. Britney started to gain more independence. Though Kevin still misbehaved more than Britney, his behavior didn't affect Sally as much because she knew it wasn't a reflection of her worth as a parent. Her change meant less response to his bad behavior, which meant less reward for Kevin—it was no longer worth pursuing.

What Now?

To close this chapter, I suggest you list all the characteristics of yourself as a parent. List the negative ones first, since they are the easiest to remember, then the positive ones.

Things about myself that I don't like in my parenting:

_____
_____
_____
_____
_____
_____
_____
_____
_____
_____

Things about myself that I do like in my parenting:

_____
_____
_____
_____
_____
_____
_____
_____
_____
_____
_____
_____

Now give each negative trait the critical parent test. Cross out any irrational and unspecific characteristics, then focus on the legitimate shortcomings. Ask God for forgiveness and guidance and strength. Then forgive yourself and start looking for ways to change. Perhaps you can take a parenting class or read one of several excellent parenting books on the market today. (I recommend *The Father Book* by Dr. Frank Minirth, Dr. Paul Warren, and Dr. Brian Newman or *Mothering* by Dr. Grace Ketterman.)

Now look at the positive list. Rejoice and pat yourself on the back. As any parent will attest, parenting is the most difficult job on earth.

14

Step Ten

Improving Your Relationship with Your Parents

I have emphasized that your present life is influenced by your family of origin (your parents and siblings). You owe your existence to this family, which makes conflict resolution doubly hard.

• •

As we did with your current family, I want you to do a family sculpture of your family of origin. Think back to a particular time when your siblings and parents were all living under the same roof. If you came from a stepfamily, include your stepparents and stepsiblings in this diagram. In the enlarged house-shaped box, following, draw a circle for every member of your family of origin. Place the circles in proximity to each other in terms of emotional closeness or distance. Write the name of the family member in the appropriate circle.

• •

Note each member's role based on the dynamics of your family unit. Write this role in the circle with the person's name. The roles you can assign include: Model Child; Troublemaker/Scapegoat; Disciplinarian/Authoritarian Parent; Nurturer Parent; Friend/Playmate Parent; Child-Parent; Peacemaker.

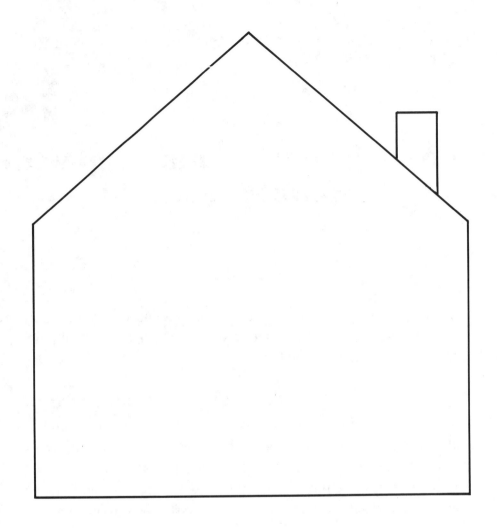

My Family of Origin Family Sculpture

If your family had at least two children, you probably will have a scapegoat/troublemaker and a model child. Most families have these two roles. If you had more than two children in your family of origin, there will probably still be just one troublemaker/scapegoat and one model child. The other siblings will fall somewhere in between these two extremes.

Let's look at Sally Dansen's family sculpture.

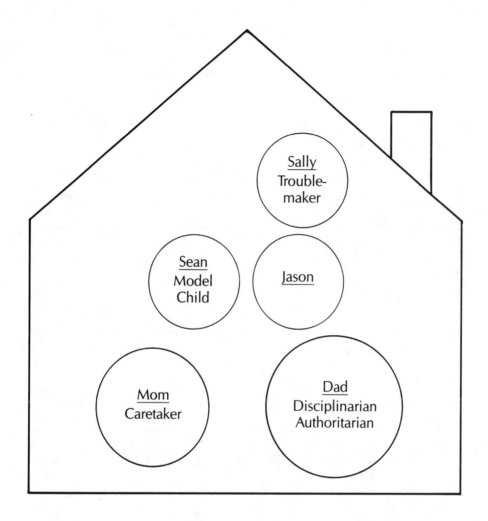

Sally Dansen's Family of Origin Family Sculpture

. . . .

Now study your own family diagram as you have drawn it. Don't erase or change anything. Your first impression is always the most accurate. Answer the following questions while looking at the diagram.

1. What's your overall impression based on this drawing?

_____

_____

_____

_____

_____

2. Which child seems to have been the closest to your parents (which circle is closest to your parents)? _____

_____

3. Was this child closer to one parent than the other? _____ yes _____ no   If so, which one? _____

4. Where did you place yourself in this diagram? _____

_____

_____

5. Were you in close proximity to either of your parents? _____ yes _____ no   If so, which one? _____
If no, why not? _____

_____

_____

6. Were you in close proximity to any of your siblings? _____ yes _____ no   If yes, which one? _____
If no, why not?_____

_____

_____

7. Which role did you play in your childhood?
   _____ troublemaker/scapegoat
   _____ model child
   _____ peacemaker
   _____ child-parent
   _____ other: _____

8. Do you notice any particular alignments in this diagram? (For example, are you and your siblings all an equal distance from your par-

ents?) _____ yes _____ no   If yes, describe the alignment. (Sally said, "My brothers are clustered around my parents. I'm out in left field all alone.") _____

_____

_____

_____

_____

9. Did you find yourself competing for your parents' attention with your siblings? _____ yes _____ no   If yes, did you win at this competition? _____ yes _____ no (Sally said at first she tried to win her parents' approval, particularly her father's, but that she gave up trying as she grew older.)

Comments: _____

_____

_____

10. Based on your diagram and your answers to the above questions, describe your relationship with your parents.

Sally had this to say about her relationships with her parents: "My relationship with my mother was very distant. I never felt I measured up to what she wanted as a daughter. She was always strict with me. I had to do my chores, or else. I had to excel in school, it was expected. Yet when I did all this, I never heard any sincere praise. It was just expected, that's all. The only times I can remember her being nurturing and loving is when I was sick. In fact, those are the fondest memories I have of my mother.

"My relationship with my father was also distant. As a child, I feared him. He really had a temper and if you didn't toe the line, he would let you know it. He seemed lots more comfortable with my brothers. If I climbed up in his lap, I could sense he wasn't comfortable with me there. He definitely ruled our house."

Now it's your turn.

My relationship with my mother was: _____

_____

_____

_____

_____

My relationship with my father was: _____

_____

_____

_____

_____

Include any stepparents you lived with: _____

_____

_____

_____

_____

_____

11. Based on your diagram and your answers to the above questions, describe your relationship with each of your siblings. Make sure to include any stepsiblings.

Sally's relationship with her brothers was fairly typical. She fought the most with her youngest brother, Jason. And because Sally was the oldest, she was usually held responsible for these fights. Sally idolized Sean, her other brother who was the middle sibling. He was the model child of the family and her parents' favorite. She tried to copy Sean, tried to be as good an athlete and student as Sean was, but she frequently fell short.

Now describe your relationship with each of your siblings.

My relationship with my sister/brother _____
was: _____

_____

_____

_____

_____

My relationship with my sister/brother _____
was: _____

_____

_____

_____

_____

_____

My relationship with my sister/brother _____
was: _____

_____

_____

_____

_____

My relationship with my stepsibling _____
was: _____

_____

_____

_____

_____

_____

My relationship with my stepsibling _____
was: _____
_____
_____
_____
_____

• •

Now that you have a picture of your family of origin system, I want you to analyze it further and find ways to improve each relationship. We'll begin with your parents.

Your Relationship with Your Parents

Just as the relationship with your children changes, so does the relationship with your parents. Your parents represent power figures in your life. Normally, they are the longest physical relationship you will have in your earthly life.

And they are the single most important role models for how you relate to others and to yourself. For instance, the way you relate with your spouse will be influenced by what you saw in your parents' interactions. As adults, our parents still have the power to invoke certain emotional responses in us that no one else can.

• •

Let's explore just what these emotional responses can be. For the purpose of this exercise, if your parents are no longer living, remember back to your last interactions. If your parents have remarried, you'll need to consider your stepparent(s) in the analysis.

1. How often do you communicate with your parents? _____
_____
_____

2. How do you feel when you talk with your mom and/or dad on the phone? (For example, I feel like I'm a child again. Sometimes I find myself wanting their protection and care. Or, I enjoy talking with them. We have a friendship more than a parent-child relationship.)

_____

_____

_____

_____

3. How do you feel after you've hung up? (For example, I get mad at myself for allowing them to control my life once again. I'm no longer a child and shouldn't act that way when talking to them. Or, I feel glad to have reconnected with them.)

_____

_____

_____

4. How often do you visit your parents? _____

_____

5. Are you satisfied with this frequency? ____ yes ____ no

6. Are your parents satisfied with this frequency? ____ yes ____ no

7. If your visits are infrequent, is it because of:
    ____ geographic reasons
    ____ financial reasons
    ____ my choice
    ____ their choice
    ____ other: _____

8. Think of the most recent visit to your parents' home. Whose idea was it for the visit? ____ yours ____ theirs

9. How did you feel on this visit? (For example, I felt like I was a child again. I felt the irrational need to please my parents. I wanted my

children to behave. Or, I felt comfortable. I enjoyed myself and so did they).

_____

_____

_____

_____

10. How did you feel after your visit was over? (For example, I got mad at myself. I let myself fall into the same trap again. Why do I let my parents control my behaviors this way? Why can't I be immune to them as an adult?) _____

_____

_____

_____

_____

11. Based on your above answers, characterize the present relationship with your mother in a few brief sentences. Is it warm, neutral, or guarded? _____

_____

_____

With your father? _____

_____

_____

_____

12. Do you see any room for improvement in your relationship with your mother? _____ yes _____ no   How about with your father? _____ yes _____ no

• •

The rest of this chapter will be devoted to improving this relationship. Unfortunately, there are hurdles to this improvement, barriers within you and within other members of your family of origin.

Hindrances to Change

One hindrance is habit. We get into the habit of relating to our parents and siblings a certain way. We have established behavior patterns over the years. In fact most of us behave as we do without being conscious of it. It is simply a matter of conditioning. Perhaps you notice yourself stepping back in time every time you visit with your family. It's probably more pronounced when you are physically in the presence of your parents.

Another hindrance is the thought processes of your other family members. If your parents were to accept change, in essence they would be admitting they did things wrong. For your siblings to change would involve their realizing their childhood wasn't what they thought it was.

In a nutshell, accepting the need to change means admitting to error, and it takes a mighty strong individual to admit a mistake. Your other family members have probably not read this workbook and, thus, have no idea what you are discovering. Parents may admit they did wrong, that they made mistakes, but it's rare that they will change their behavior patterns. (Don't hold this against your parents. Remember what you've had to go through in this workbook to change your own behavior patterns.)

You may even resist change. To change your behavior may invoke a fear of abandonment in your inner child. Why? If we change our behavior, our inner child gets a message from our critical parent that our parents will no longer be like or love us. It's irrational, but we believe it. If we change our behavior, which until now assured our love and nurturance, will this love and nurturance cease?

That leads us to another hindrance—the critical parent voice. This voice will sabotage every step toward change. Its goal is to make you unhappy. Any attempt you make toward recovery and maintenance of your inner child will be hampered by this voice. Watch out for it. It might even get at you using a spiritual disguise.

Misguided spirituality is also a hurdle to your renewed relationship with your parents. We are taught from an early age to honor our mother and father. And we fear that examining our upbringing is somehow dishonoring them. Nothing could be further from the truth. In fact you could hardly honor them more than by going through pain and suffering to have a better relationship with them in the end. I've often stated, we are not "parent bashing" with these exercises. Our goal has never been to blame and condemn our parents. Rather, we are looking at our childhood as objectively as possible and, hopefully, learning from this analysis how to better our adult lives.

With the above knowledge in hand, I want you to put on a psychotherapist's hat the next time you visit your folks. Take this workbook with you. Try to objectively analyze what happens while you're there. Then record the events as they unfolded. Put them down under "incident" in the following chart.

. . . .

PARENT RELATIONSHIP CHART

Incident:_____

_____

_____

_____

_____

My Feelings: _____

_____

_____

_____

Inner Child Messages:_____

_____

_____

_____

. . . .

Next, record your feelings in response to the event or behavior. Finally, see if you can discern the messages your inner child might be receiving from this event.

Dorothy took this chart with her on a visit to her parents. She could almost predict what would happen when she walked in the door, based on past visits.

"Good to see you, Mom," she said as she opened the door. She gave her mom a hug.

"Good to see you, Honey," her mom answered. "My, but it looks like you've put on weight. Having trouble with your dieting?"

Dorothy clenched her teeth. "No, Mom. I'm trying the best I can. It's not easy."

"I know, Sweetie." Her mom patted her cheek. "Well, come in and see your father. He's in the den."

Based on this event, Dorothy filled in her chart.

• •

PARENT RELATIONSHIP CHART

Incident: Mom commented on my weight (like always) as soon as I greeted her.

My Feelings: I felt terrible, hurt, and extremely self-conscious. Any enthusiasm I had for the visit was gone.

My Inner Child Messages: I felt like a failure, like I had really messed up. I couldn't control myself. I felt I was really, really weak and bad.

• •

Which player do you think is speaking to Dorothy with these inner child messages? _____

Do they seem irrational and unspecific? ____ yes ____ no   The obvious answer is the critical parent.

Interestingly, Dorothy's mom did not make Dorothy feel this way; Dorothy's critical parent voice did.

Our inner child receives a negative message or feels bad at something our parents do or say because our critical parent reacts to the event.

Put another way, one person's behavior cannot cause another person to feel a certain way. Unfortunately this is the excuse we all use, and by using it we give another person responsibility for our feelings. This is simply not the way it is. God did not design it this way.

To the alcoholic who claims he drinks because of his wife, I ask, "Did she restrain you and pour the alcohol down your throat?"

Dorothy still has the option to tell her mother that such comments hurt her feelings. We all have this right. The point I'm trying to make is that we shouldn't gear our behavior or feelings around what others tell us. It's up to us to counteract any hurting statements with good parent responses. However, this does not remove our right to tell another person our feelings.

Dorothy wants to improve her relationship with her mother so she needs to cast her critical parent voice aside and only listen to her good parent voice. Likewise, this should be your goal.

Dorothy began to rationally evaluate this interchange between her and her mother. Her chart now looked like the following:

• •

PARENT RELATIONSHIP CHART

Incident: Mom commented on my weight (like always) as soon as I greeted her.

My Feelings: I felt terrible, hurt, and extremely self-conscious. Any enthusiasm I had for the visit was gone.

My Inner Child Messages: I felt like a failure, like I had really messed up. I couldn't control myself. I felt I was really, really weak and bad.

The Player Speaking: The critical parent.

Adult Messages: Well, this is Mom's opinion. She thinks I'm overweight. Further, it seems she's obsessed with my weight because she asks about it every time I visit. Even though she's a very important person in my life, she's only one person out of five billion in the world, with one opinion. Does that mean it's valid? Not really. Who judges what is the right weight for me? I do. I'm the one whose opinion matters on this score. And my opinion doesn't need to be swayed by hers. If I decide personally that I have put on too much weight, it will be my decision, not because of my mother's opinion. I still love her, but I don't have to accept her opinion.

Good Parent Messages: I'm worthwhile and significant in the Lord's eyes. He doesn't care how much I weigh. I haven't messed up. I'm okay. God loves me and my inner child just the way we are.

• •

Remember, *The good parent voice is always the direct opposite of the critical parent voice* (just as God and Satan are opposites). *It is an affirming and validating message while the critical parent message is judgmental and critical.*

Now go back and complete your chart, using Dorothy's as a model.

• •

PARENT RELATIONSHIP CHART

Incident: _____

_____

_____

_____

_____

My Feelings: _____

_____

_____

_____

Inner Child Messages:_____

_____

_____

_____

_____

_____

_____

_____

The Player Speaking:_____

_____

Adult Messages:_____

_____

_____

_____

Good Parent Messages:_____

_____

_____

_____

• •

I further recommend that you continue to keep this workbook with you when you visit your folks, since it will be difficult for you to maintain this pattern of thinking without a reminder.

Again, your goal should not be to change your parents' behavior. Instead, your goal is to change your response to their behavior. The net result will probably be very little change in the way they act toward you. However, the way you respond to them will change drastically.

To close this section, list all the wrong you feel your parents have done to you.

• •

MY PARENTS' SHORTCOMINGS

Mom	Dad
_____	_____
_____	_____
_____	_____
_____	_____
_____	_____
_____	_____

_____   _____

_____   _____

_____   _____

_____   _____

_____   _____

• •

If you have stepparents include them in this list. Now go back and forgive your parents for each shortcoming. I don't recommend confronting your parents with this forgiveness because they may not realize these traits as shortcomings.

Instead, do it symbolically. If you can't remember how to do this, reread chapter 9. If one or both of them were perpetrators for the injuries your inner child received, you should have forgiven them earlier in this workbook for those wounds.

This list, however, covers all the little things you felt were wrong in your upbringing. Learn to see your parents' shortcomings as *their* weaknesses rather than internalizing these shortcomings as negative messages to your inner child.

Now is the time to resolve these issues once and for all. Go on with a newly enhanced relationship with your parents, much as God expects when He says: "Honor your father and your mother, that your days may be long upon the land which the Lord your God is giving you" (Ex. 20:12).

Improving Your Relationships with Your Siblings

"Have you seen Anne recently?" Dorothy's mom asked her when Dorothy was over for dinner.

"Yeah, just last Wednesday. Why?" she answered.

"Then you don't know about Earl's promotion, do you?"

"No. Did he get a raise?"

"Closed a big deal, apparently. Anne says they'll move to a larger house in Cloverdale."

"Figures," Dorothy said.

"Too bad you can't find a nice guy like Earl," her mother commented.

Dorothy didn't answer. Instead she scooped out another helping of mashed potatoes.

Your Relationship with Your Siblings

The family structure is such that all siblings compete for the attention of their parents. Sibling rivalry is no myth; it's a fact of life. My experience has shown that birth order can affect this parental attention.

The firstborn child usually falls short of parental expectations and may become the troublemaker/scapegoat. This is because the parents are learning with this first child and tend to have higher ideals. Then, later children come along. Because parental expectations become more realistic, one of these later siblings is more apt to be a model child. Each child then begins to fulfill his or her inherited role.

The scapegoat child never quite fits in the family. He or she is usually in the most trouble. The scapegoat is given the unconscious message that he or she is falling short of expectations by the parents and is inferior to the model child.

The model child always seems to excel. He or she usually makes the best grades, does the best in sports, music, or other activities. The model child goes on to college, graduates, marries the perfect spouse, and has the perfect family.

In my experience, the model child is no happier than the scapegoat. However, the scapegoat is usually the one most open to change and therapy because he most believes he needs it.

Inventory Your Siblings

List all your siblings and yourself in the following chart. Include any step-siblings you lived with a great deal of time. Along with their names, list any roles they played (scapegoat, model child, peacemaker, child-parent). If you can, list them in the order of birth, from firstborn to last and include yourself in the list.

. . . .

MY SIBLING INVENTORY

Firstborn: _____ Role: _____

Second-born: _____ Role: _____

Third-born: _____ Role: _____

Fourth-born:_____ Role: _____

Fifth-born or Stepsibling: _____ Role: _____

. . . .

After you've completed this inventory, look back at the family sculpture you did at the beginning of chapter 14. Summarize your relationship with each sibling in the spaces provided below.

• •

Firstborn: _____

_____

_____

_____

Second-born: _____

_____

_____

_____

Third-born: _____

_____

_____

_____

Fourth-born: _____

_____

_____

_____

Fifth-born or Stepsibling: _____

_____

_____

_____

• •

Fill in something for every sibling.

Pick out the sibling you are closest to emotionally (not necessarily on a positive basis). Answer the following questions.

Sibling's Name: _____

1. What adjectives describe this sibling? (For example, is this person successful, trustworthy, dependable, playful, irresponsible?)

_____

_____

_____

2. How do you feel about this sibling today? (For example, I feel closer to my sister today than when we were growing up. She's a close friend.) _____

_____

_____

3. What feelings does this sibling invoke in you during your interactions? (For example, I sometimes get very defensive when I talk with my sister, as if I have to justify why I made some decision.) ___

_____

_____

4. Can you recall a time during your childhood that you felt these same feelings in the presence of this sibling? ____ yes ____ no   Describe the circumstances: _____

_____

_____

_____

Whatever you felt in the past is probably what you feel now as you relate to this sibling. The inner child messages are probably also the same.

Now go back and complete these questions for every sibling with whom you had a close relationship (positive or negative). I've provided room for one more below. Make copies of this form as needed.

· ·

1. What adjectives describe this sibling? (For example, is this person successful, trustworthy, dependable, playful, irresponsible?)

_____

_____

_____

2. How do you feel about this sibling today? (For example, I feel closer to my sister today than when we were growing up. She's a close friend.) _____

_____

_____

3. What feelings does this sibling invoke in you during your interactions? (For example, I sometimes get very defensive when I talk with my sister, as if I have to justify why I made some decision.) _____

_____

_____

4. Can you recall a time during your childhood that you felt these same feelings in the presence of this sibling? ____ yes ____ no Describe the circumstances: _____

_____

_____

· ·

Dorothy's sister, Anne, was the one who always excelled in school. Anne was married with two children. Dorothy was single. Dorothy had problems. She struggled with her weight and social relationships. The two sisters lived in the same town so they kept in frequent contact.

Which role do you think Dorothy's sister, Anne, plays in the family?

_____

Which role do you think Dorothy plays in her family of origin?

_____

_____

It's fairly obvious that Anne is the model child while Dorothy is the troublemaker/scapegoat. As Anne grew into an adult, she joined rank with her parents against Dorothy. Unfortunately this is very common for model child roles; they will tend to parent the scapegoat in their adult lives. So Dorothy not only received powerful inner child messages from her parents but also from her sister.

I asked Dorothy to keep track, in a notebook, of the incidents she encountered with her sister. At Dorothy's next session, she had the following event to recall.

"My sister lives clear across town from me," she explained. "I have to drive through a bad part of the city to get to her house. On this particular day, I knew I had to get gas. I was planning on stopping at my regular station on the way. I got there and the pumps were out of order.

"I decided to try and get gas at another station. Well, I couldn't find any station on the way. I ran out right in the most horrible section of town.

"Now I had just seen the movie *Grand Canyon,* so I panicked. What was I going to do? I knew I needed to get to a phone to call for help, but I couldn't see a phone anywhere and I didn't want to leave the car. I just sat there and cried. Eventually, a man came up to my car and knocked on the window. Luckily, he was helpful and called a tow truck.

"By the time I finally got to my sister's house, I was distraught and she was worried sick."

"What'd your sister say to you?" I asked.

"She was glad I was safe, of course," Dorothy answered. "Then she asked what happened. And I told her."

"What'd she say then?"

"I don't remember her exact words, but it was something like, 'Same old Dorothy. How could you be so careless? Didn't you think to plan ahead and have enough gas? You could have been hurt. You've got to be more careful next time.'"

"How'd you feel when she said these things?" I asked.

"I felt really stupid, like I'd been caught in another mistake."

"What do you think your inner child heard from this interchange?"

"I suppose that I'm stupid, I made a dumb mistake. I am dumb and I am bad. I can't take care of myself. Statements like those."

"You're learning," I said. "Which player do you suppose is making those statements to you?"

"Well, I was dumb. I should have been more careful. So maybe it's my good parent instructing me."

"Be careful," I warned Dorothy. "You are so used to hearing these types of statements, you believe them. From what you've told me, you were the one in the family who always messed up. And just like any other childhood conditioning, you've grown used to hearing this broken record. You even unconsciously expect it. But that doesn't mean these statements are correct. If you examine each of these statements, you'll notice the critical and judgmental tone of them. Which player uses this tone?"

"The critical parent?" Dorothy asked.

"Exactly," I answered. "That's whom you've been listening to most of your life. And this player does not have your best interest in mind. What we need to do now, just as we did with your parents, is teach you how to hear the good parent voice."

As Dorothy did, recall a recent incident with the sibling you have the most emotional involvement with. Summarize what happened.

• •

Recent incident with my sibling, _____ (name):

_____

_____

_____

_____

_____

_____

_____

_____

_____

_____

_____

_____

What were your emotional responses to this event? I felt

_____

_____

_____

_____

_____

List what types of messages your inner child received from this inter-action. My inner child heard _____

_____

_____

_____

Do these statements sound familiar? _____ yes _____ no   Have you heard them over and over throughout your childhood? _____ yes _____ no   Are they judgmental, critical, and demeaning? _____ yes _____ no   If you could answer yes to one of the questions above, chances are you are hearing these messages from your critical parent. Obviously, if you hope to have an improved relationship with this sibling, you need to change this.

• •

Calling on the Good Parent Voice

When you have an incident such as the one you described above, try to substitute your critical parent messages with an adult message (a rational explanation for the event and your feelings) and a good parent message (from the Holy Spirit).

When Dorothy did this after her incident with Anne, her statements were:

Adult response: Anne is right, I did make a mistake. I should have had gas before I drove through that part of town. But that doesn't mean I will always make mistakes. Nor does it mean I'm less of a person. I am only human and will make mistakes. It's through God's grace that I can learn from these mistakes. Next time I'll be sure to have a full tank before I drive to Anne's house.

Good Parent messages: Anne's words do not measure my self-worth; God does that. He accepts me as I am, faults and all. I am worthy. I am significant. I am a good person. I am only human and will make mistakes—and that's okay.

Now it's your turn. Substitute adult and good parent messages for your critical parent messages from your sibling incident. _____

_____

_____

_____

_____

Good parent message: _____

_____

_____

_____

_____

Dorothy also realized something very significant from this analytical process. Anne was behaving toward her based on Anne's own conditioning as the model child. She found that she started to feel sorry for her sister. She prayed Anne would break out of this role and become as free as Dorothy had become.

It's a spiritual and psychological truth that the more we see others as merely acting out of their own inner difficulties, the more we see them as victims (possibly of their own critical parent voices), just as we are. And we ultimately learn to understand and forgive their behavior. The net result is the beginning of a society that is more forgiving and understanding as individuals take responsibility for their feelings rather than blaming others.

Sounds like the perfect society, doesn't it? It begins with each individual. God uses this truth to show us empathy and compassion for others, rather than jealousy and competition.

Try and do this same exercise for each sibling.

The Last Step

The crucial last step toward enhancing your sibling relationships is forgiveness. In the space provided below, list each wrongdoing you felt your sibling committed against you. Beside each wrongdoing, indicate whether you think the act was committed because of your sibling's role in the family unit.

• •

LIST OF WRONGDOINGS FROM MY SIBLING

_____ (name)

Wrongdoing	Product of His/Her Assigned Role
_____	___ yes ___ no
_____	___ yes ___ no
_____	___ yes ___ no
_____	___ yes ___ no
_____	___ yes ___ no
_____	___ yes ___ no

Wrongdoing	Product of His/Her Assigned Role
_____	____ yes ____ no
_____	____ yes ____ no
_____	____ yes ____ no
_____	____ yes ____ no
_____	____ yes ____ no

• •

Remember, no one has to continue acting out their roles, or their scripts. Each person is responsible for his or her own actions, including each of your siblings. You are not excusing their behavior, just forgiving it.

Now go back and methodically forgive your sibling for each one of these wrongdoings. You can do this either in person or symbolically. Symbolically is the easiest.

For this I suggest you sit somewhere quiet and private. Mentally picture the special place you described in chapter 9. Visualize you and God leading your sibling to this place. Now picture the three of you sitting together, conversing. Read off the list above and forgive your sibling for each wrongdoing. Then read the following statement to your visualized sibling:

"I want to pursue a new relationship with you, not based on the past, but based on spiritual truths that our Father shows us. Out of my love for you, I want to build a stronger and more sincere relationship with you. I know you don't have to change or even recognize these truths. But I also know if I change, our relationship will. From now on, I am starting a new relationship with you."

Before you leave this place, thank God for His presence and guidance in your life.

If you choose to do this in person with your sibling, keep these points in mind.

1. Your sibling has not gone through this workbook. He or she will have no idea what you're talking about. Your sibling may even think you're crazy.

2. Your sibling may respond to you with his or her same old behavior patterns. Remember it's hard, very hard to change the family system. He or she may discount what you're trying to say.

If you encounter either of these reactions from your sibling, I highly recommend you end the interaction as quickly as possible. The validity of what you are saying or feeling does not depend on another's response. We are not trying to change your sibling's behavior, rather your response to that behavior.

Make sure you do these exercises for each sibling. Keep this workbook with you whenever you visit them. It will help to remind you to call on the good parent when you receive a critical parent message. It will also help remind you that your siblings' behavior may be more a product of their childhood conditioning than rational thought.

Dorothy realized that her sister's behavior was largely influenced by her model child role. As I mentioned before, Dorothy found compassion for her sister with this knowledge. She attempted to forgive Anne in person since the two sisters were very close. When Anne couldn't understand what Dorothy was saying, Dorothy ended the interchange as lovingly as possible. She then forgave Anne, symbolically, at another time.

16

Improving Your Relationships on the Job and in Social Settings

"Now that we've examined your family and personal relationships, how are things going at work?" I asked Phil Sanderling.

"Fine," Phil answered. "I don't think I have any problems there. My boss can be a witch sometimes. Otherwise, a job's a job, you know."

"You have a female supervisor, I gather?" I asked.

"Yeah, recently promoted into her job."

"Tell me more about your relationship with your boss," I said.

"What do you mean?" Phil asked.

"How do you feel around her? Do you have a comfortable working relationship? Those kinds of things," I said.

"Well, to tell the truth, I try to avoid her most of the time. She's very authoritarian. Just last week I had an evaluation session with her. She raked me over the coals. So I guess I don't really have a comfortable relationship with her."

"Help me remember. What's your mother like again?" I asked.

"She's always involved in my affairs, sometimes too much so. In my teen years, I felt almost strangled by her. Even nowadays, I think she's too interested in my life. She's always trying to fix me up with a daughter of one of her friends. I love her very much, but she doesn't know when to let go. What's all this got to do with my job anyway? You showed me how this creates my approach-avoidance behavior in my relationships with others. Don't tell me this affects my job too."

Work Relationships

I didn't tell Phil this outright. Instead, I led him through some exercises so he could discover it on his own. Below are the same questions Phil answered. Answer them as best you can.

• •

1. How well do you get along with your boss? (For example, we have a professional relationship. He's very intimidating. I relate to him on only a polite, superficial basis. Strictly business. Or, she's very supportive. I can go to her with any problem and she will help me see the solution.)

_____

_____

_____

_____

_____

2. Do you enjoy talking with him or her? ____ yes ____ no

3. Do you find reasons not to talk with your boss? ____ yes ____ no

4. Do you avoid him or her? ____ yes ____ no

5. What qualities does your boss possess that cause these reactions within you? (For example, he's very authoritarian. He's also very egotistical. He's almost like a dictator. He makes people jump and he seems to like this power.) _____

_____

_____

_____

_____

6. Are you free to express your feelings to your boss? _____ yes
_____ no   If so, does he or she acknowledge your feelings? _____ yes
_____ no   Why or why not? _____

_____

_____

_____

_____

7. Does your boss seem concerned with only facts and thus relates to
you on only a business, information-gathering level? _____ yes _____ no

8. Does your boss relate to others in your office or workplace the
same way as he or she does with you? _____ yes _____ no   If no, why
do you think he or she treats you differently? (For example, my boss
treats me differently because I seem to make the most mistakes [or
because I'm a man/woman]. He's always on my case.)

_____

_____

_____

_____

9. Are there any similar characteristics between your boss and your
parent of the same sex? _____ yes _____ no   If so, what are they? (For
example, my father was authoritarian and a disciplinarian. What he
said went. My boss is the same way.) _____

_____

_____

_____

_____

_____

10. Do you find that your reactions to your boss are similar to your
reactions to your father (if you have a male boss) or mother (if you
have a female boss)? _____ yes _____ no   If yes, what are these reac-

tions? (For example, I react just like an admonished little boy. I feel sorry for my mistake and I feel compelled to work all the harder to do better in my boss's eyes. I guess I'm intimidated by him/her and try to win his/her approval just like I did with my mom/dad.) _____

_____

_____

_____

_____

If no, does your boss remind you of someone else you've had an interaction with? ____ yes ____ no   If yes, describe that other person.

_____

_____

_____

_____

11. Based on the above answers, how would you characterize your working relationship with your boss? (For example, now I see that I have almost a father/son relationship with my boss, without the love and affection.) _____

_____

_____

_____

• •

As you could probably guess, the relationship we have in the workplace can mimic the relationship with our family of origin.

Pseudo-Family

You are completely accountable to your boss for your salary, your work schedule, and your performance. It's very easy to equate this relationship with that of your parents. Thus, any unresolved issues you have with your parents will tend to be played out in the workplace with your boss.

For example, a male who has a female boss may have difficulty accepting her authority over him if his mother was a submissive person. Conversely, a male who had a domineering mother will tend to play out typical approach-avoidance behavior with a female boss (Phil Sanderling fell into this category).

The same is true for a female employee. Any unresolved issues she has with her father will tend to transfer over to her male boss. And any problems she has with her mother will tend to reflect in her relationship with a female boss.

Relationships in the workplace tend to mirror family dynamics with the emotional responses that go along with these behaviors. Although we do, at times, react emotionally in the workplace just as we do at home, the workplace cannot accommodate this response. The business world does not accept these emotional behaviors as proper. What is left is lots of unfinished business and problems being dealt with totally on the surface between outer selves, but controlled by how the inner children feel.

It's almost like being on a Ferris wheel for the first time. You don't know what is coming next; sometimes it's thrilling and sometimes it's downright terrifying. Only the operator can control where you're going, not you.

As an example of how this works, let's look at a colleague of mine. Being a social worker, he operates in a predominantly female-oriented profession. Thus, he's had many female bosses. He told me recently that every time he was rated on his performance, he reverted back to when his mother reprimanded him for doing wrong. He began to dread conferences with these women.

Then it finally dawned on him that he was projecting his mother into these other women authority figures. Once he was able to separate his family issues from his workplace, things got much better.

Just as bosses will tend to reflect your parents, so coworkers will mirror your siblings. They may vie for your boss's attention and approval. Any issues you suffer with your siblings will tend to carry over in your relations with your coworkers.

Thus, the first technique I use to improve workplace relations is to separate these relationship issues from your family ones. Let's begin with your boss.

SEPARATION TECHNIQUES

Identify which parent most resembles your boss: _____

2. Now characterize the relationship you have with your boss. (Is it a warm, close relationship or a distant, impersonal one?) _____

_____

_____

_____

3. Are the two similar? _____ yes _____ no

4. Can you discern what messages your inner child might be receiving from your boss's actions? _____ yes _____ no   If yes, list them below. (For example, I'm stupid. I mess up and make big mistakes. I rarely do anything right.) _____

_____

_____

_____

5. If you can't come up with any inner child messages, try and recall the most recent confrontation you had with your boss. Briefly summarize the incident below. (For example, I was called into his office yesterday. He mentioned a contract I had made a mistake on. I immediately got defensive.) _____

_____

_____

_____

_____

6. Now list any feelings you had as a result of this incident. (For example, I felt like I had really messed up. How could I have been so stupid? I didn't feel good about myself and it bothered me the rest of the day.) _____

_____

_____

_____

_____

7. Finally, based on these feelings, how do you think your inner child felt? (For example, my inner child got the "I am bad" message. I am not a worthy person.) _____

_____

_____

_____

_____

8. Now look closely at these inner child messages. Are they similar in any way to the ones you listed in chapter 14, which you heard from your parents (especially the same sex parent as your boss)? _____ yes _____ no If yes, what are these inner child messages? _____

_____

_____

_____

If no, do these inner child messages reflect ones you've heard from other people in your life (your spouse, one of your siblings, an adult authority figure in your childhood)? _____ yes _____ no

9. More than likely the inner child messages from your boss are similar to ones you've heard from your parents or other authority figures in your life. And it's a good bet that these inner child messages are coming from your critical parent.

• •

My colleague heard the following inner child messages from his female bosses: "You're not okay. You aren't very smart. You can't take care of yourself. You're not responsible."

His bosses didn't even mean to send these messages. But that's what he received. And that's also what he received from his mother while growing up.

Our first technique will be to discount these incorrect inner child messages and substitute good parent ones. Before we begin, we need to pray and ask God to make Himself present in our good parent voice.

As with our parents, Scripture advises us to respect persons in authority. But doing so does not mean that we think of ourselves as less. We also need to keep in mind the following points:

1. Your boss is not your parent. Your boss is a whole separate being with an entirely separate history and family from you.
2. Your job performance and your self-worth are two entirely different things. When you work at a job, sometimes your performance will be negatively evaluated by your superiors. This evaluation is never a reflection of your value as a person. This is difficult, but you must separate your self-worth from what is told you by your boss.

The identity of your inner child has nothing whatsoever to do with who you are in your career. Your inner child doesn't care if you're the company president or employee of the month. All your inner child cares about is how you feel about yourself and about him or her. Once you achieve this perspective, you are free to accept criticism constructively and objectively, and look at ways you can improve.

It's absolutely wrong to equate poor job performance with poor self-worth. You are a good, worthy person, regardless of how you perform on the job. Unfortunately, the world judges our worth by our appearance to the world. One of the more common ways we present ourselves to the world is through our jobs. This is primarily why so many homemakers have such a hard time with self-esteem. Society discounts this profession. It's also why many retirees become depressed. Their self-worth was tied to their occupation. When the occupation ceases, so does their self-worth.

To counter these incorrect messages to your inner child, you need to call on your good parent voice. Let's take a specific example and see how this works.

Phil Sanderling told me that at his latest meeting with his boss, he totally discounted everything she had to say.

"What was your inner child hearing at this meeting, do you think?" I asked.

"Well probably the same message: I'm worthless. I make mistakes. I'm not a good human being," Phil answered.

"And because you were hurt, you completely rejected everything your boss told you. Is that correct?" I asked.

"That's correct," Phil responded. "I get tired of always being evaluated by her."

"And you also get tired of always being evaluated by your mother, isn't that right?"

It took Phil a while to see this. After a few sessions, he agreed. "You know you're right. I really do see my mother in my boss."

"And this projection is what is hampering your relationship with your boss. Are you willing to try an exercise with me?"

"Sure. Guess I've nothing to lose."

"And everything to gain," I added. "Tonight when you go home, take two chairs and face them toward one another. Picture your boss and your mother sitting in one chair—sort of a composite boss-parent. Sit yourself down in the facing chair and address this composite boss-parent.

"Next, spill your feelings, all your anger, your resentment, everything. Tell this composite being how you really feel about it. You might say:

'You make me feel small and insignificant. You make me feel stupid. I feel like I can't do anything right in your eyes.'

"After you've told this composite boss-parent how you feel, bring in another chair to your circle. Then, mentally separate your mother from your boss. Put them in separate chairs. To your mother, say what you need to say. If there are still hurts you feel from your mother, acknowledge them. Finally, forgive your mother for these hurts as you did before. Lovingly dismiss your mother from this circle. Take one of the chairs out of the circle.

"Then address your boss, who is now separate from your mother. Say whatever you want to say to your boss. If you can't think of something to say, read this statement.

"'I feel you have, at times, not treated me with the respect I deserve as an adult and employee. You do not have the control over me that my mother does because you are a separate person. I will relate to you only on an adult-to-adult basis. I will love you as a fellow human being and will respect you. I will listen to your guidance, but I will not allow myself to become emotionally involved with you as I do with my parents.'

"Close your discussion with your visualized boss by forgiving her for any wrongdoings you felt were done to you at her hands. And then pray for your boss to learn the skill and knowledge to be a good supervisor to you."

Phil went home and did this exercise. He related to me that he felt much better in his office afterwards. You should also perform this exercise if you have trouble with your boss. If you don't, great! Just keep this in mind if a problem ever does arise. It also works with coworkers.

Coworkers

Coworkers tend to resemble our siblings as bosses do our parents. Thus the same dynamics for improvement of these relationships apply.

• •

1. Identify a coworker you have conflict with on a regular basis below. This conflict can be stated or unstated. What person in your office or workplace causes you the most trouble, other than your boss?

_____

_____

_____

2. Does this person remind you of a sibling or another person of consequence in your life? ____ yes ____ no   If yes, who? _____ If no, skip to number four.

3. What characteristics are common between this coworker and your sibling or other person (competitiveness, joins rank with your boss

the way your sibling joins rank with your parents)? _____

_____

_____

4. What inner child messages do you think you hear from the actions and behaviors of this coworker? (For example, if this coworker joins ranks with your boss, do you hear the same critical messages: You're not performing up to standard; you make mistakes; he or she loves me more than you?) _____

_____

_____

If this coworker reminds you of a sibling, the inner child messages should be similar to what you hear from this sibling.

5. Now perform the same separation exercise you did for your boss. (If you can't identify any similar individual to this coworker in your past, use only two chairs and skip the next paragraph.)

Tell the coworker-sibling composite everything you feel about him/her. Spill out all your feelings. Then separate your sibling from this coworker and put him or her in a separate chair. Deal with your sibling as I suggested you deal with your parent. Then lovingly dismiss him or her from this conversation and remove the third chair.

Address the coworker you've visualized in the second chair using the following as a guide.

• •

"_____ (name) I know you are not my sister or brother (or other significant individual). You are separate from him or her. I know you do not determine my self-worth and significance as a human being. We may have had our differences in the past, but I am willing to proceed from this point forward in a new, enlightened relationship with you. I know we need to work together and that we will still have differences. But I will learn, with the grace of God as my help, to not take these differences personally rather to relate to you on a purely rational basis. I will not allow your behaviors and actions to control my feelings."

• •

6. After this exercise, pray to God, thanking Him for his presence in your interchange with this visualized coworker and ask Him to reveal the good parent voice to you.

7. Now go back and cross out the inner child messages you listed in number four. Substitute them with good parent messages and list them below.

Good parent messages: _____

_____

_____

_____

_____

• •

Some of them you might want to list are, "I'm significant and worthy as a person. No matter what this other person tells me, I am still loved by God and I still love my inner child. I am okay inside."

Let's end this exercise with a prayer:

Dear God,

If I see a way I can improve the relationship with this person, please help me do so. I still have to work with this person, who is a child of God just as much as I am. Help me to remove my resentful and angry glasses and see them as You do.

Serendipity

One great bonus to looking at others through inner child eyes is that you see how they might be controlled by what their inner child is feeling. As I said before, this gives you insight and compassion. Your boss or your coworker might be treating you a certain way, based on what happened to them in their family of origin. Needless to say, emotions are present in the workplace whether we recognize them or not.

Whenever the old feelings start to nudge their way back inside you, do this exercise again, separating your boss from your parent or your coworker from your sibling. Deal with your boss or coworker as one adult to another.

There is one thing you should be aware of though. Doing these exercises once will not resolve all your relationship issues in your workplace. Total separation of emotions from the workplace is impossible because we are all emotional beings. This workbook will help you understand those emotions and put them in their proper place so you can carry out your business in a professional manner. You will likely still get upset with your boss or coworkers, and you may have to do these separation techniques several times. Don't expect to be free of your feelings. In fact, I don't want you to be free of your feelings. I just want you to better understand them.

Social Relationships

Social relationships are relationships we have with friends and acquaintances met in everyday life. It's interesting that we sometimes measure our self-worth more by our social relationships than by any others because social relationships are usually primarily between our outer selves. Except for childhood friends, we do not, typically, have a long history with people in our social lives.

These are the people we meet in the grocery store, at our child's school, and in church. We start out on a casual, surface level with them, and instantaneously start comparing ourselves with them.

Since they are new to us, we hide away our inner child and show only the outer self. We tend to communicate with small, polite chit-chat. Yet, God didn't put us all on this earth by chance. We meet and interact with the people around us for a reason.

"I will never take another person for granted," a recovered cancer patient said once. "Now whenever I meet someone and see an opportunity for meaningful conversation, whether that person is standing in line at the bank or at the bus stop, I grab that opportunity. Coming close to death does that to you. You suddenly realize the blessing of being around other human beings. And you feel a profound respect and love for other people."

This patient is describing what some call a "transcendent" perspective. With a transcendent perspective comes the recognition of what is important in our lives. Some feel that transcendence is the ultimate lesson we are on this planet to learn.

Our goal with social relationships should be the same as the cancer patient's—to never take another human being for granted and to develop a profound love and respect for other people. In order to obtain this, we have to learn to trust our social relationships and emerge from the "one outer self comparing itself to another outer self" mind-set. As with every other relationship, there are hurdles to this one.

The Hurdles

1. *The outer self relationship.* It's easy and predictable. We need take no risks by exposing our inner child. Instead, out of habit, we seek to stay on the surface level with others. Habits are hard to break.

2. *Fear of vulnerability.* Vulnerability is the very foundation of intimacy. If we can't allow ourselves to be vulnerable, we can't achieve an intimate relationship with others. Many of us fear a deep friendship with others, because we don't like our inner child. And we feel if others could see who we really are, they wouldn't like us very much either. Have you ever heard the saying: "I wouldn't join a club that would have me as a member"? A wounded inner child is at the root of this.

3. *Measure of self-esteem and status.* Similar to our working place relationships, we measure our self-esteem and status based on these social relationships. Thus, to risk losing a relationship by showing our inner child would

mean to risk losing self-esteem and status. This is especially prevalent in the church. We have a tendency to compare ourselves to others in the Body.

The only way to jump these hurdles is by establishing a secure, positive relationship with yourself as I discussed in chapter 11.

• •

AN INVENTORY OF YOUR SOCIAL RELATIONSHIPS

1. List all the friends you interact with on a regular basis.

1. _____

2. _____

3. _____

4. _____

5. _____

6. _____

7. _____

8. _____

9. _____

10. _____

Are you satisfied with the number of friends in your life? ____ yes ____ no   If no, why not? _____

_____

_____

If you answered no, why do you think you don't have many friends? (Is it because you don't feel you're worthy of others' time and energy? Or is it because you haven't found many people with whom you like to be?) _____

_____

_____

_____

2. Think of one friend you really enjoy being around. Why do you enjoy socializing with this person? (For example, she's in the same situation as I am. We can share a lot of the same experiences.) ____

_____

_____

_____

_____

How would you characterize your relationship with this friend? (For example, close. I can tell her anything. Or, a surface friendship. We just have a good time together with no stresses or pressure.) _____

_____

_____

_____

_____

3. Think of a person with whom you feel uncomfortable. What things about this relationship make you feel uneasy? (For example, I always feel like I can't measure up to him. He's more successful than I. After I've been with him, I feel negative about myself.) _____

_____

_____

_____

How would you characterize this relationship? (For example, it seems very surface-oriented and one-sided. He does most of the talking while I do the listening.) _____

_____

_____

_____

4. What differences do you notice between this relationship and the friendship you described in number two? (For example, I can't be the real me with this person like I can with my neighbor. I'm afraid that I

wouldn't measure up and this person wouldn't want to have me as a friend anymore.) _____

_____

_____

More than likely, the relationships you're the most uncomfortable with are the ones that precipitate critical parent messages to your inner child.

5. What are the inner child messages you receive from the relationship you described in number three? (For example, I'm not good enough. I'm not smart enough. I'm not worthy of this person's friendship.) _____

_____

_____

_____

_____

Which player do you think is stating these messages to your inner child? _____

Messages that we receive from social relationships, such as "You're inferior, you're lacking, she or he is better than you are, you're not good enough" are the broken-record style and tone of the critical parent.

6. What is it about this person that triggers your feelings of inadequacy or inferiority? (Is it material possessions or personal qualities?)

_____

_____

_____

_____

• •

Each of these qualities needs to be given the validity and rationality test. We do this by calling up the voices of the adult and good parent within us.

Let the Adult Be Heard

The adult analyzes each critical parent message to see if it's valid and rational. For example, if you believe a friend of yours is a better spouse than you are, what does that really mean? Can this be quantified? What is a better spouse? This statement is neither valid nor rational.

What if you see another person as a better daughter than you because of the way she seems to treat her elderly parents? Is this rational and valid? The adult voice would say no. Just because this person seems to be more actively involved in her parents' lives does not mean she is a better daughter to her parents than you are to yours. You are still loved by God and saved in His eyes. Thus, you are just as good a person as anyone else.

The key here is that we receive very powerful inner child messages from our social acquaintances because we are always consciously and unconsciously comparing ourselves to these other persons. Whenever comparisons enter the picture, the critical parent's judgment results.

Calling up the Good Parent

The best way to call on your good parent voice is to ask for God's help because it is through your good parent (the Holy Spirit) that God lets Himself be heard. You may use the following prayer as a guide or make one up on your own:

Lord,

Thank You for giving these other people their possessions and traits. Thank You, Lord, for blessing them. Lord, I've been remiss. I've let my inner child hear invalid and irrational messages. And I've let my inner child believe these incorrect statements. I need Your help and guidance in sorting through all this. Reveal Your truth through the Holy Spirit and good parent voice. Thank You, Lord, for helping me to this point. Help me gain mastery over these relationships with others. And help me to come closer to a transcendent relationship with all Your children.

When you call on your good parent voice, remember the following:

- Long before you or anyone else owned any possessions, or were even born, Jesus died on the cross for us to be validated, for us to enter the kingdom of heaven. The development of currency and material possessions has not altered the effect of His act. Scripture teaches us: "So the last will be first, and the first last. For many are called, but few chosen" (Matt. 20:16).
- The enemy, our critical parent voice, through which Satan works, wants us to feel insignificant and inferior to others. Our enemy may mask itself into believable statements, but they are always false.

We know by now how the critical parent disguises itself in very subtle, but damaging messages to our inner child. We've examined these inner child messages through our adult voice. Now we need to counteract these messages with our good parent voice.

Good Parent Messages for Your Social Relationships

Think of good parent responses to each inner child message you wrote in number five on page 261. For example, if you heard the inner child message, "She's a better daughter than I am because she's more active in her parents' lives," your good parent counter would be, "She may be involved more with her parents than I am, but I am still loved by God. He doesn't require me to be a more active daughter to earn His acceptance because His love for me is unconditional and unearned."

In cases such as duties to our parents or even duties to our church, the Lord wants us to look for acts we are *convicted* to do. We must follow our spiritual conviction in our family and church life. At no time do these acts subtract from or add to our personal self-worth in His eyes.

• •

Now, write out your good parent responses to your specific critical parent messages from number five.

_____

_____

_____

_____

_____

_____

_____

_____

_____

• •

Once you've replaced every inner child message with a statement from the Holy Spirit through the good parent, you can do this same exercise for every social relationship you wish to improve. But you must be aware that sometimes we are indeed judged by others.

I was in church the other day and observed a couple in the service wearing jeans and T-shirts. I immediately judged. "How could they be so disrespectful as to dress like that for the Lord's service?" I thought. But then the good parent voice and conviction came through. They weren't disrespectful; they were freer than any other person in the congregation because they were not compelled to follow a certain dress code for the approval of others. They were secure enough to come as they were to worship the Lord.

It is never correct for us to judge others. Scriptures are very clear on this: "Therefore you are inexcusable, O man, whoever you are who judge, for in whatever you judge another you condemn yourself; for you who judge practice the same things" (Rom. 2:1).

But we are all imperfect. We make mistakes. We have to realize that sometimes people will judge us. We will be looked down upon by certain individuals. However, this behavior is only their opinion. It does not mean that their assessment of us is accurate and valid.

If someone is truly being condescendent, your inner child messages from the critical parent voice will be especially strong. But with God's help you should be able to overcome them with the loving good parent voice.

17

Today Is the First Day
of the Rest of Your Life

"Guess what?" Phil said.

"What?"

"I've asked Gina to marry me."

"Wonderful!" I shook his hand. "How'd it feel popping the big question?"

Phil grinned, "It was real tough. Lots of those critical parent messages were flowing through my mind. But I managed to stop them and hear the good parent voice. It worked, Ken!"

"I'm glad," I responded. "I remember the time I asked my wife to marry me. I didn't know about all this inner child business then. It's a wonder she accepted."

"To be honest, I had my doubts at the beginning of therapy. It just sounded too simple, too easy. All I had to do was ask for the good parent voice and presto it appeared," Phil commented.

"It is a very simple concept, even though it takes a lot of work to get to this understanding. Right?" I asked.

"Right," Phil agreed. "I didn't mean it was easy. It was hard! I almost gave up several times. I had to examine lots of things about myself and my family—painful things. In the end, though, it was worth it. Going to come to the wedding?"

"You bet," I answered.

Your First Day

Of the relationships discussed in this workbook, with whom are the most difficult?

_____

_____

_____

_____

_____

_____

_____

_____

For each of these relationships, indicate if you have noticed any improvement since you began this workbook. _____ yes _____ no   List the relationships below, along with the improvements you've noticed.

Relationship: _____ Improvement: _____

_____

_____

Relationship: _____ Improvement: _____

_____

_____

Relationship: _____ Improvement: _____

_____

_____

• •

What's still a problem with your relationships and how can you help to resolve it?

• •

Relationship: _____ Problem: _____

_____

Possible Resolution: _____

Relationship: _____ Problem: _____

_____

Possible Resolution: _____

Relationship: _____ Problem: _____

_____

Possible Resolution: _____

• •

There will be relationships that continue to be difficult, just as life will continue to be difficult. For these, you must grieve. You cannot change others, only yourself.

This was the hardest realization for me. For most of my life, I treated relationships like appliances. If they worked, fine; I thought nothing more about them. If they didn't, I felt an overwhelming desire to fix them. Because of this, I wouldn't let others see my inner child. I didn't feel good about my inner self and, thus, to show it to another meant I would risk breaking a relationship.

This dynamic controlled me so much that I would go out of my way to try and repair any relationship that had negative feelings. The other people in my life even became conditioned to give me responses that I wanted. Responses such as, "Yeah, I was mad at you. But now I'm not." Once I heard things were okay, I felt better.

Rediscovering my inner child has taught me to accept relationships as purely human—nothing more, nothing less. I have come to expect other people to be no more than human—fallible, imperfect, and controlled, to a certain extent, by their own pasts.

The bottom line is that once we see each other in this light, we can be more accepting of our emotions as well as others'. We finally have the knowledge needed for true, intimate relationships. The only way this can happen is by first validating our inner selves so that we will not be threatened by negative emotions from another person.

For those relationships that have improved, you must rejoice and celebrate. All your hard work has paid off.

Phil Sanderling improved his relationship not only with Gina, now his fiancée, but he also improved his relationship with his mother and his boss. That's the payoff for getting to the root of the problem. Once your inner child is healed and validated, most outer relationships improve.

That's why I suggest you keep this workbook with you throughout your life. This book is only your guide, though. Daily communication with God is what strengthens us. Jesus said: "Ask, and it will be given to you; seek, and you will find; knock, and it will be opened to you. For everyone who asks receives, and he who seeks finds, and to him who knocks it will be opened" (Matt. 7:7–8).

Help won't come automatically. You have to ask for it. The only way to ask is to first know you need help.

Progress Check

I like to ask my clients for an evaluation at the end of their therapy. This way I can see, but more importantly they can see, the progress they've made. In some cases, like Phil Sanderling, it's remarkable.

In others, like Ellen and Sally, it's downright miraculous. Sally Dansen had been through a horrible, traumatic childhood. There was much to be healed within her. She made amazing progress. Her relationships with her husband and children all improved. She was able to get her compulsions and fears under control with the help of support groups; she was on the road to becoming a functioning adult.

Ellen, the widow who lost contact with her son, also made remarkable recovery from her codependency. She joined a support group and was able to maintain her recovery with their help. A particularly poignant example of

Ellen's metamorphosis through Inner Child therapy is exhibited in the following interchanges I had with her in my office:

"I've had a dream about my special place, that country road I told you about earlier," she told me. "In the dream I see someone walking down the road. It's a young person and she's bent over as if carrying a heavy load. Another person, an older woman, walks up and joins this young person. She takes the child's hand and together they walk down the road. As I observe them, the younger one slowly drops her load and stands up straight. Then I see the two persons merge. This person runs and frolicks like a happy child. She watches the butterflies, throws rocks, and laughs at the birds."

"Who do you think this person is?" I asked Ellen.

"I don't know."

Several sessions later, Ellen had the answer.

"I had the dream again," she explained. "This time I recognized the person as my inner child. It is me running and playing along that road."

"And how do you feel about this part of you?" I asked her.

"I feel good about this part of me. I feel hopeful. I feel totally acceptable and worthy before God as this person. I love this part of me."

Ellen found that once she was secure in her relationship with herself, her inner child, she did not have to pursue relationships with others to prove her self-worth. Today, Ellen has a few close relationships with other people to round out her life, but she does not cling to them. She is secure in God's love for her.

Before I ask you to rate your progress, read Sally Dansen's response.

"The insights I've gained through this therapy are obvious to me now. I blamed myself for many years for what happened to me as a child. I didn't like myself very much and treated myself very poorly. I know now that's why I was so unhappy. I have learned to accept myself and to love my inner child with God's help.

"But I still have much to learn. I am still afraid to open up to others. It's getting better, but I have a long way to go. I have difficulty forgiving others and myself for the pain I've suffered. It was very difficult to forgive my uncle for the pain he caused. I know I need more guidance and strength from God on this. But I also know that I will be okay, because I am okay inside."

• •

1. What insights have you gained about yourself while completing the exercises in this workbook? _____

_____

_____

_____

_____

_____

_____

_____

_____

_____

2. What have you learned? _____

_____

_____

_____

_____

3. What do you feel you still need to learn? _____

_____

_____

_____

_____

• •

This workbook is only one approach to happiness and relationship building. It is not the only way. Nor is it the Divine way. Keep in mind, Inner Child therapy isn't for everyone. I've had many patients who could not visualize or see an inner child no matter how often I tried these exercises. For those individuals, I usually shift to other therapeutic methods.

I've primarily focused on unconscious thought processes in this book. I also recommend two other books which emphasize healthy, conscious thought patterns as a complement to my therapy. They are *The Lies We Believe* and *The Twelve Best Kept Secrets for Living an Emotionally Healthy Life*, both by Chris Thurman.

By now, you should be able to recognize the critical parent voice, its motives, and the repetitive tone of its messages. It should be fairly easy to recite them.

• •

Write out the tired and worn words of the critical parent messages below.

_____

_____

_____

_____

_____

You should be just as familiar with the tone of the good parent voice. It speaks universal truths that apply no matter what the situation. Can you think of the few, common truths of the good parent voice? They are: _____

_____

_____

_____

_____

_____

• •

I've provided some of these truths below. The ones we should all memorize.

The Truths of the Good Parent Voice

There's no better way to end this workbook than by restating these truths. In fact, you might want to copy them onto 3 x 5 cards and carry them with you.

1. I'm okay. I was made okay by the blood of Christ. I am validated by God's unconditional and unearned love for me. I am significant.
2. I am a good person. I have strong self-worth. God loves me as I am. I am a worthy person inside. My feelings are valid. My thoughts are valid. My inner child is valid.
3. I am a human being. I will make mistakes. I am not perfect. Further, God doesn't expect me to be perfect. He loves me despite my faults. When I make mistakes, I can ask for His forgiveness and the conviction to learn from them.

Change is possible. "Jesus looked at them and said to them, 'With men this is impossible, but with God all things are possible'" (Matt. 19:26). My prayers go with you as you continue your journey.

About the Author

Ken Parker maintains a full time practice at the Minirth-Meier, Tunnell and Wilson Clinic of Austin, Texas. In addition to presenting seminars and workshops, he also leads small workgroups on "Reclaiming Your Inner Child" at the Austin Clinic. He is a licensed marriage and family therapist and holds a master's degree in social work from the University of Texas at Austin.